The Brainiest INSANIEST ULTIMATE PUZZLE BOOK!

Robert Leighton, Mike Shenk, and Amy Goldstein

Workman Publishing • New York

Acknowledgments

We'd like to thank the talented artists who illustrated many of the puzzles in this book: Ron Barrett, Dave Clegg, Rob Collinet, Daryll Collins, Bob Fingerman, Michael Gelen, Gary Hallgren, Stuart Immonen, Terry Kovalcik, Bill Ledger, Phil Marden, Steve Mellor, Jim Paillot, Leah Palmer Preiss, Kevin Rechin, Sally Vitsky, and Sam Ward. Thanks also to the editors of *Disney Adventures* magazine, where most of these puzzles first appeared. And finally, thanks to puzzle testers Kyle Leighton and Evan O'Donnell.

■ ■ ■

All of the puzzles in this book first appeared in *Disney Adventures* magazine, except Ticket or Leave It (p. 22), Downpour (p. 126), In the O Zone (p. 82), The Name of the Game (p. 116), Treat or Trick? (p. 89), Veg Out (p. 100), Your Move (p. 134), It All Adds Up (p. 153), and the Scavenger Hunt (fold-out).

Library of Congress Cataloging-in-Publication Data is available.
ISBN-10: 0-7611-4386-6   ISBN-13: 978-0-7611-4386-4

Cover design by Paul Gamarello
Interior design by Paul Gamarello and Dove Pedlosky
Puzzle design by Puzzability

Workman Publishing Company, Inc.
225 Varick Street
New York, NY 10014-4381
www.workman.com

Printed in the United States of America
First printing October 2006
10 9 8 7 6 5 4

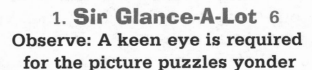

Contents

. . .

Still have puzzle fever? Take a crack at the Scavenger Hunt at the very end
of the book—complete it, and you'll earn the Certificate of Achievement!

Introduction

This is no ordinary book. For one thing, you don't write in an ordinary book. We heartily encourage you to write all over this one. For another thing, an ordinary book has chapters to be read in order—otherwise, you might find out "who done it" before you know what's been done. This book has sections where the order doesn't matter—dive in wherever you like!

The sections are hosted by different characters who will present different kinds of puzzles, so if you have a favorite type, you'll know where to look. The book begins with Sir Glance-A-Lot, who presents the picture puzzles, followed by the Riddle Green Men, who ask questions of all sorts. Alice in Wanderland will take you through the mazes, The Wordman of Alcatraz is in charge of the word puzzles, and Sherlogic Holmes handles the logic and reasoning section. Finally, there's FrankEinstein, who looms over the section with the book's toughest puzzles. (In the other sections, we haven't said what's easy or what's hard because different people are better at different kinds of puzzles.)

Like we said, this is no ordinary book. No ordinary book would make a point of telling you what to do if you get stuck. Novels aren't known for offering advice to people who can't follow the story. Atlases don't say how to find your way home if you get lost, and dictionaries don't tell you how to look up a word if you can't already spell it (although they probably should). So just in case you find yourself stuck along the way, here are some tips to keep in mind:

1 **Read (or reread) the instructions.** Why are some of the boxes different colors? What do the arrows mean? Should I cross off these words as I use them? Read the instructions, and you'll find out. Sometimes a puzzle will have a bonus message that you won't find unless you know how to look for it. Other times, two puzzles may look similar to each other but have different rules for solving.

2 **You don't always have to solve everything in the order it's given.** If you get stuck solving from top to bottom or left to right, just jump somewhere else and work your way out from there. Also, some puzzles have two parts (like many in the Riddle Green Men section, which reveal the answer to a riddle when you're done). If you can solve some—but not all—of the first part, maybe you can use what you know to figure out some or all of the final answer. Then you can use that information to get the parts you skipped over.

3 **Stop solving and come back to the puzzle later.** If you find yourself trying the same thing over and over again, put the puzzle down. Sometimes all you need to do is come back later and the answer will suddenly pop out at you. (Your brain keeps working on it even though you're doing other things.)

In case you're permanently puzzled (or just want to check how you did), the answers are all in the back of the book. There you'll also find a special fold-out Scavenger Hunt that will have you searching cover-to-cover to solve one more super-puzzle, *and* a tear-out Certificate of Achievement that you can earn by solving the Scavenger Hunt.

As puzzle writers, we think that the best puzzles are not at all like tests. They're sometimes tricky, often challenging, and always fun.

But never ordinary.

Sir Glance-A-Lot

Observe:
A keen eye is
required for
the picture
puzzles yonder

8

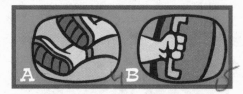

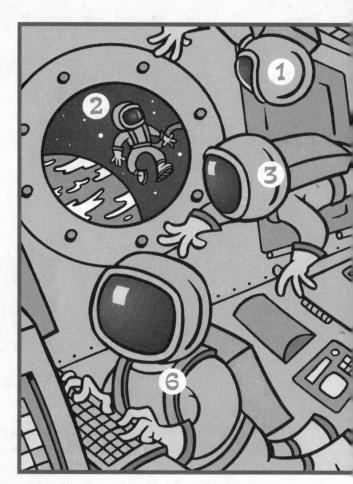

Brrr!

This chilly scene contains 17 things that start with the letters BR. For example, the two boys are brothers. Can you find the other 16 items?

Answers, page 169.

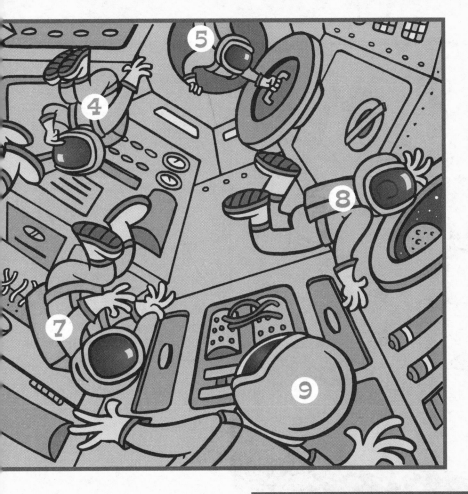

It's Astro-Logical

There's plenty of work to be done in the new space station. But is everybody doing their share? One of these astronauts is actually sound asleep. The views seen by eight of the astronauts are shown at the far left. Determine what each one sees by matching the views (A–H) to the astronauts (1–9). The leftover astronaut is the goof-off!

Answers, page 169.

9

Tree's Company

Somewhere within this grid of leaves are specific shapes, shown at the top, made up of all four kinds of leaves—with each kind of leaf appearing once within each shape. The shapes appear in the grid exactly as shown, without any rotation. See if you can find them all.

Answers, page 169.

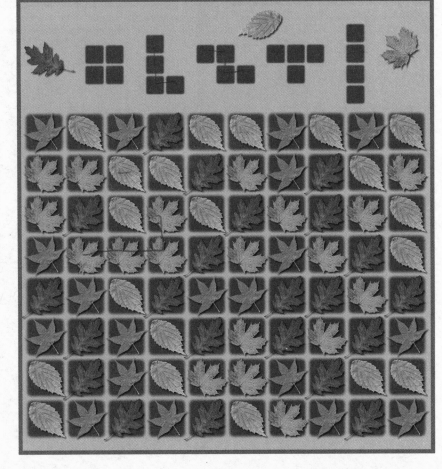

Look! Up in the Sky!

This kite contest began with pairs of kites that matched exactly in color and design. After one kid let go of his string, he got a new kite that matched one of the other pairs. Can you search the sky and find the 12 pairs of matching kites, the only one that's one of a kind, and the group of three?

Answers, page 169.

10

Trick or Trade

Each of these trick-or-treaters has ended up with a piece from a costume that belongs to someone else shown. See if you can reunite each kid with the costume part he or she is missing.

Answers, page 169.

"The vision of the octopus is so keen that it is studied by men and ladies of science to this day."

Out to Lunch

It's tough to order here—nearly everything in this diner is out of order. How many of the 24 mistakes in this scene can you find?

Answers, page 169.

Instant Replay

These two pictures may seem identical, but look again! There are actually 14 differences between the picture on the left and the one on the right. How many can you catch?

Answers, page 169.

12

Double Take

This picture contains seven shapes that appear in two different places. That foot pedal on the trash can, for example, also appears as the dog's ear—turned, but the same size, shape, and color. Can you find the other six pairs of shapes?

Answers, page 169.

13

Snow Business

Snowflake Inspector #51 is on the lookout for any snowflake whose six sections do not all match perfectly. The inspector will approve only two of these snowflakes. Can you find them and spot the mistakes in the other five?

Answers, page 169.

Simply Smashing

Only two of these smashed reflections are exactly alike. Can you tell which?

Answers, page 169.

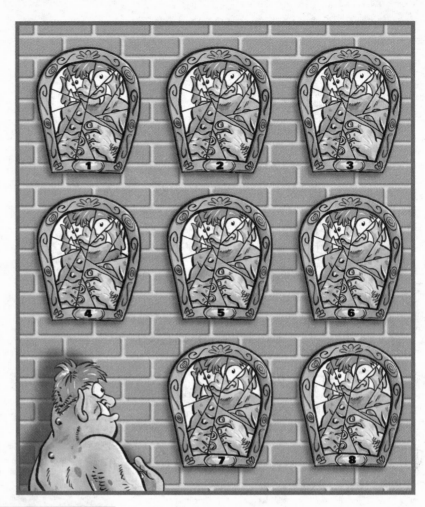

Even Steven

Scattered around this scene are three things that rhyme with each of these numbers: two, four, six, eight, and ten. Can you be counted on to find them all?

Answers, page 169.

Foiled Again!

One of the gathered suspects in this scene stole the leftovers from last night's dinner, and it's up to you to solve the mystery. First answer all the detective's questions by examining the scene, then find your answers in the grid of letters. Once you've circled all of the correct answers, read the "leftovers" (all the letters not circled) from left to right, starting at the top row, to reveal how the detective solved the mystery.

Answers, page 169.

CASE FILE #DA004 --
THE MISSING LEFTOVERS

```
B U T R H R E M M A H E P A
A I M E N S H A R K T L S V
S E R B O W L I N G A E W I
K A S O R B C D A D S U G O
E V I T C E T E D S H T S L
T K S C R A L E A E D O D I
H A A O A R R L I N C O L N
C F O R K D G N A K D E G D
```

1. What did the thief leave behind on the empty plate? _____
2. What month is shown on the calendar? _____
3. Who is the only person sitting down? _____
4. What item is leaning against the bookshelf? _____
5. What article of clothing was left on the back of the sofa? _____
6. Who does the carved bust depict? _____
7. What is the wrapped item that the mailman just brought? _____
8. What activity is depicted on the trophy? _____
9. What kind of pet lives in this house? _____
10. What kind of container are the flowers in? _____
11. What did the carpenter drop on his way into the room? _____
12. What kind of animal is mounted on the wall? _____
13. What is the maid wearing on her leg? _____
14. What important feature did the artist leave off his portrait? _____
15. What item is propped up against the wall in the hallway? _____
16. What is in the gardener's hand? _____
17. What are the mailman, artist, and carpenter all wearing on their faces? _____
18. Which person tracked mud across the floor? _____

Wrap Group

Santa gave these elves five rolls of wrapping paper and five spools of ribbon. He told them to use every combination of paper and ribbon so that no two of the 25 presents were wrapped the same way. The tired elves have just one box to go. Which combination of wrapping paper and ribbon should they use to complete the set?

Answers, page 170.

Insiders

If you were tiny, you could fit inside some great places playing hide-and-seek. Here are six familiar spots that no normal-size person has ever seen from the inside out. Can you identify each place?

Answers, page 170.

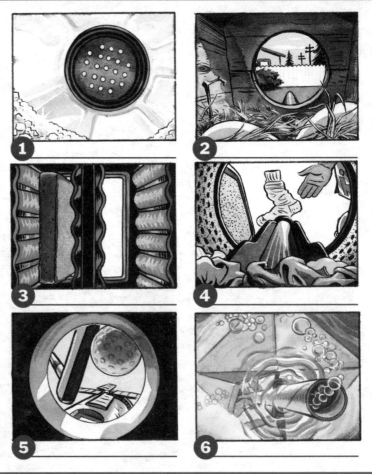

Junked Mail

Emily sent this postcard from her vacation at Mount Rushmore. There are mistakes everywhere—like that misspelling of "Rushmore" right on the card's front. Look at both sides of the postcard and see how many of the other 18 mistakes you can spot.

Answers, page 170.

17

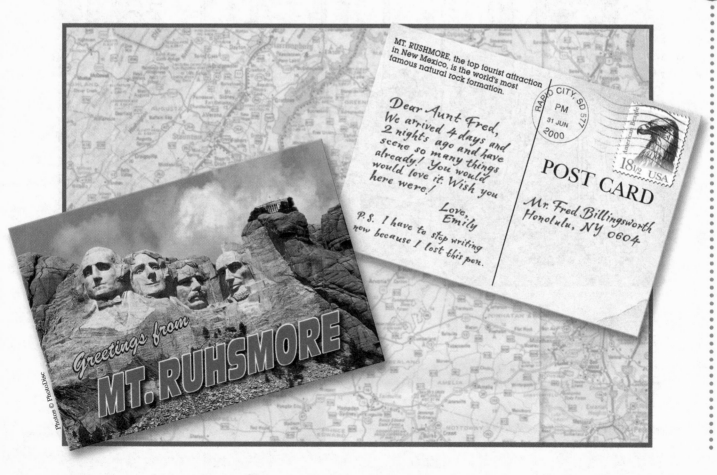

"So sensitive is the human eye that it can perceive a candle on a dark night from the distance of one mile."

It's All Downhill From Here

There are 22 things wrong in this ski lodge scene. How many of the mistakes can you find?

Answers, page 170.

Flipping Out

Only two of these skateboarders are exactly alike. Can you tell which?

Answers, page 170.

Hot Lines

These kids have been in the sun too long, and it shows . . . everywhere except in the two areas where each was wearing something. Look carefully at the patterns on each kid, and see if you can match them with two items on the blanket.

Answers, page 170.

Spare Change

These two pictures are completely identical in every way. Wait—strike that. There are actually 17 differences between them. How many of them can you pin down?

Answers, page 170.

Snowed In

This picture contains seven shapes that appear in two different places. That snowdrift in the window, for example, also appears as the white part of the boy's hood— turned, but the same size, shape, and color. Can you find the other six pairs of shapes?

Answers, page 170.

Bat Attitude

There are 25 hidden bats haunting this Halloween scene. How many of them can you scare up?

Answers, page 170.

21

22

Ticket or Leave It

There are 22 things wrong in this movie theater lobby. How many of the mistakes can you find?

Answers, page 171.

Roundup

Welcome, pardner, to the Circle Ranch, where near about everything ends with "O." You can start with rodeo, f'rinstance. Can you find 19 other things ending in "O"?

Answers, page 171.

One, Two, Tree

This tree was originally decorated with nothing but pairs of matching ornaments. After one broke, it was replaced with an ornament already on the tree twice. Can you search the tree and find the 16 pairs of matching ornaments, the only one that's one of a kind, and the group of three?

Answers, page 171.

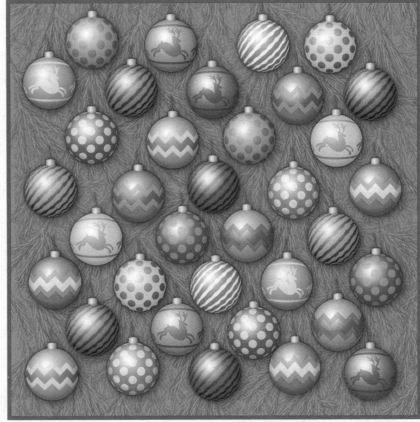

Get Real!

A busy counterfeiter has been churning out worthless copies of some very valuable items. Fortunately for the police, he manages to make a mistake in almost every one of his forgeries. In each group, study the original and then see if you can find the one perfect copy and spot the mistake in each of the other four phonies.

Answers, page 170.

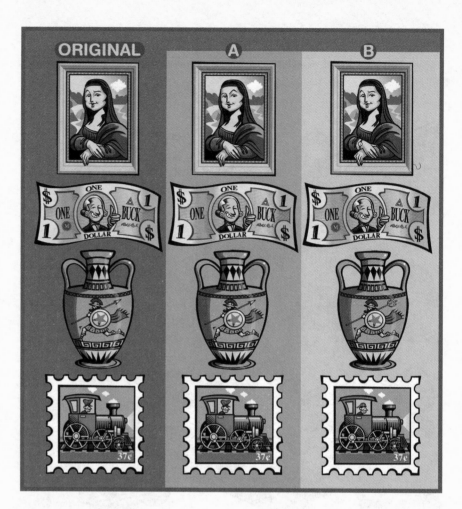

ORIGINAL   A   B

24

Triangle Trio

Three pictures are hidden in this tangle of lines. To find them, color in every shape that has three sides. When you're done, identify the three pictures and see if you can figure out what their names have in common.

Answers, page 171.

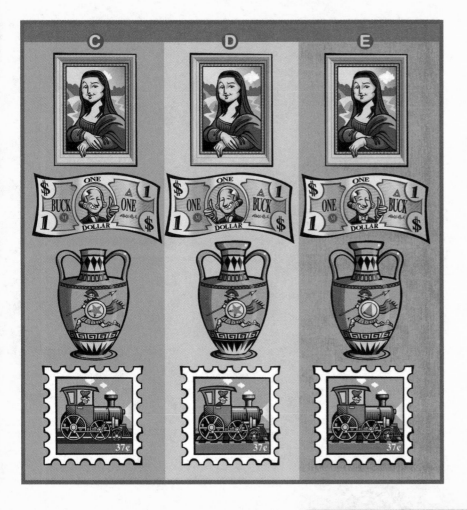

Rhapsody in Boo

There may not be bats in our belfry, but there sure are ghosts in our attic. They feel right at home, too, since there are 13 items up there that contain the letter sequence BOO. Can you find them all?

Answers, page 171.

Look Out Below

You're not seeing double—and that's the problem. The reflections in this frozen pond don't exactly match what's happening on its surface. Can you find 16 differences between the reflected images and the real thing?

Answers, page 171.

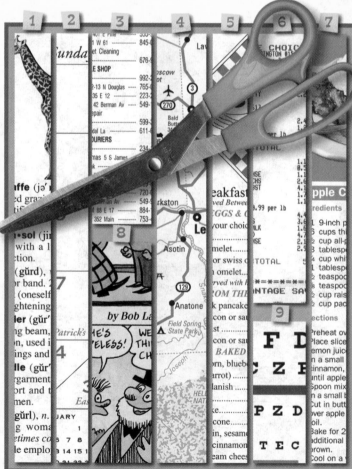

Cut It Out!

You have your work cut out for you here. The nine snippets shown come from familiar kinds of reading material that you may have never looked at this closely before. Can you tell what types of things they are?

Answers, page 171.

27

Birds of a Feather

Can you find seven pairs of identical birds and spot the only bird that has no match? Birds do not need to face in the same direction to be identical, so look instead for identical features and colors.

Answers, page 171.

Dinner's on Me!

Only two of these toppling burger platters are exactly alike. Can you tell which?

Answers, page 171.

The Dr. Is In

Doctor's orders: Find 17 items in this waiting room that begin with the letters DR. For example, that bottle on the table in front has a dropper. Can you find the other 16 items?

Answers, page 171.

Hide-and-Squeak

Is there a mouse in the house? Actually, there are eight mice hiding in this scene. The small views below show what each mouse sees from its hiding spot. Can you figure out where each mouse must be hiding in order to see each view?

Answers, page 172.

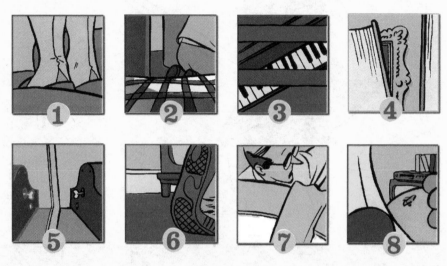

1

2

3

4

5

6

7

8

"Verily, a mirror does not show how you look to other people, for it flips your image from right side to left."

Mirror, Mirror

There are at least 27 differences between the scene on the left and its mirror reflection on the right. For example, the direction of the plane is reflected incorrectly. How many other differences can you spot?

Answers, page 172.

It's No Use!

Each object here is missing something important. Take a good look and see if you can tell what isn't there.

Answers, page 171.

Band Over Backward

It looks like practice makes imperfect for this struggling garage band. There are 12 things wrong with this jam session scene. How many of them can you find?

Answers, page 172.

Picture __6__
DO __G_____
DO _____
DO _____

Picture ____
RE_____
RE_____
RE_____

Picture ___
MI _____
MI _____
MI _____

Picture ____
FA _____
FA _____
FA _____

Picture ____
SO_____
SO_____
SO_____

Picture ___
LA _____
LA _____
LA _____

Picture ____
TI _____
TI _____
TI _____

Drawn to Scale

Each of these seven pictures represents one of the notes of the scale: DO, RE, MI, FA, SO, LA, and TI. But which is which? Look carefully and you'll see that each picture contains three things that start with the letters of one of those notes. For example, Picture 6 contains a dog and two other DO words. Can you fill in all the other words?

Answers, page 172.

Space Case

Meglak purposely bought a spaceship that didn't look like anybody else's, and now she can't find it in this galactic parking lot. To help her, look carefully at all the spacecraft and find the 12 matching pairs. When you've matched every pair, the one spaceship left unmatched is Meglak's.

Answers, page 172.

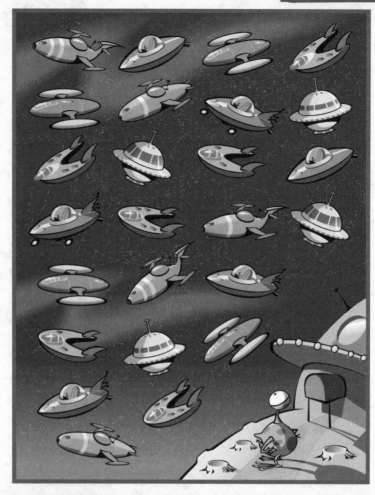

33

Eye Bogglers

Can you recognize these everyday items from their extreme close-ups?

Answers, page 172.

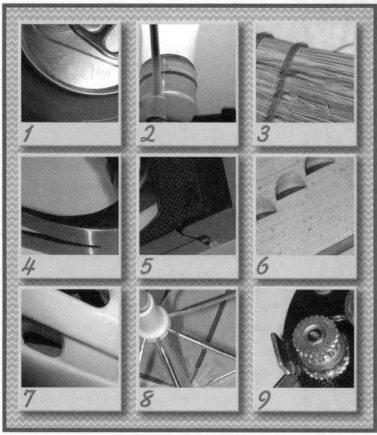

Call of the Wild

If you look carefully at this wintry scene, you'll find that bear, beaver, elk, fox, moose, and rabbit are all hiding somewhere in the picture. Can you find them all?

Answers, page 172.

34

Look Twice

There are 12 pairs of matching shapes hiding among these pictures. That bald man's spoon, for example, also appears as the baseball player's cap—turned, but the same size, shape, and color. Can you find all 12 pairs of shapes? Each picture will be used twice.

Answers, page 172.

Animal Crackers

There are 25 things wrong in this pet shop scene. How many of the mistakes can you find?

Answers, page 173.

36

Haunted Hike

Which haunted house do the trick-or-treaters live in? The small pictures to the right show the views they see as they make their way through the neighborhood—in the order they see them. By comparing these views to the large picture on the top, you can map their route and find the one house whose front door they don't pass—that's the house they live in. Starting note: They have just trick-or-treated at the house they're standing in front of.

Answers, page 172.

Garden Party

After the occupants of this home placed four store-bought garden gnomes on their front lawn, their property was invaded by real gnomes, who thought they saw a party going on. The four fake gnomes are identical to each other, but each of the eight real gnomes has one difference that sets him apart from the others. Can you spot all the differences and tell the real gnomes from the models?

Answers, page 173.

37

Tic Tac Show

Scattered around this scene are four things that rhyme with "tic," four that rhyme with "tac," and four that rhyme with "toe." Can you find them all?

Answers, page 173.

TIC	TAC	TOE

Riddle Green Men

Riddle puzzles
and other unidentified
flying questions

| 8 | 4 | 24 | 15 |
| 5 |

| 10 | 16 | 21 | 3 | 26 |

| 17 | | 12 | | 23 |

| 11 | | 19 | | 1 |

| 25 | 20 | 9 | 2 | 6 | 14 |

| 13 | 18 | 7 | | 22 |

Crunch Time

This puzzle has two parts. First, name the eight pictures and figure out where to put the words in the crossword. Second, transfer the letters from the crossword to the numbered boxes at the bottom to get the answer to the riddle. Hint: Start by filling in the only six-letter word.

Answers, page 173.

Why did the robot eat the neon sign?

1	2	3	4	5	6	7
8	9	10	11	12	13	14	15
16	17	18	19	20	21
22	23	24	25	26

Cross-Outs

To solve this puzzle, first read the list of directions and cross out any pictures that apply. In each step, you will delete either two or three pictures. When you're done, two pictures will remain. Identify their names in order from top to bottom to get the answer to the riddle.

Answers, page 173.

What does Dracula keep in his medicine chest?

1. Cross out any picture whose name rhymes with **GHOUL**.

2. Cross out any pictures whose names are the same.

3. Cross out anything whose name can become the word **SCARE** by changing one letter.

4. Cross out two pictures whose names have their letters in reverse order of each other.

5. Cross out anything whose name contains the letters O, G, R, and E in any order.

6. Cross out anything you put candles in.

Why are rock concerts such cool places to be? Because . . .

A Piece of the Action

To get the answer to the riddle, look at the nine individual pieces and find them in the large picture. (Careful, some pieces have been rotated.) When you find a piece, write the letters showing where it came from—the row first (blue diamond) and the column second (green diamond). When you've found them all, those letters will spell out, in order, the answer to the riddle. The location of the first piece has been filled in for you.

Answers, page 173.

ABC Ya Later!

Follow the eight instructions to cross out letters in the alphabet shown. (Some letters will be crossed out more than once.) When you're done, there will be five letters left. You'll get a surprise answer word when you follow the final instruction at the bottom.

Answers, page 174.

1. Cross out each letter that rhymes with "bay."
2. Cross out each letter that forms a common English word when it's put in front of "our."
3. Cross out each letter that appears in the numbers of a clock that uses Roman numerals.
4. Cross out each letter that is immediately to the left or right of the X on a standard keyboard.
5. Cross out each letter that appears only once when you spell out all the numbers from 1 to 12.
6. Cross out each letter that appears twice in a row in any word in Clue 2.
7. Cross out each letter that is the last letter in the name of more than one month.
8. Cross out each letter that is the first letter of the name of a coin with a value higher than a penny but lower than a half dollar.

A B C D E F G H I J K L M N O P Q R S T U V W X Y Z

Take the leftover letters in order, and you should be able to write the answer below.

☐ ☐ ☐ ☐ ☐

42

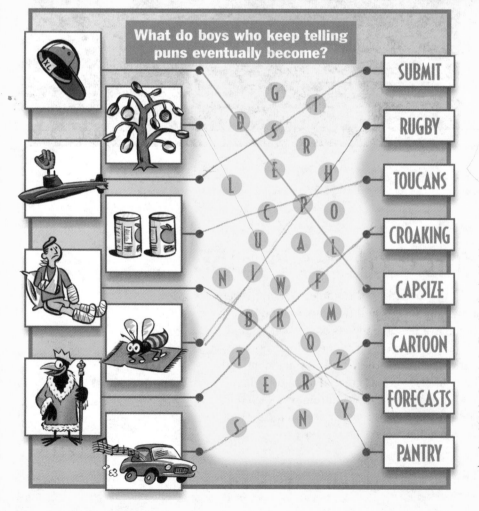

What do boys who keep telling puns eventually become?

SUBMIT

RUGBY

TOUCANS

CROAKING

CAPSIZE

CARTOON

FORECASTS

PANTRY

Just Say the Word

To find the answer to the riddle, draw a straight line from each of the words on the right to the picture on the left that is a punny illustration of the way that word sounds. The word CAPSIZE and the picture showing "cap size" have been connected to get you started. Each line you draw will cross out some letters. When you're finished, read the leftover letters in order, from top to bottom, to get the answer to the riddle.

Answers, page 174.

Look Both Ways

To solve the riddle, use the clues to fill in as many answer words as you can. The answers are the same both across and down, so enter each word in both directions to complete the puzzle. When you've filled in all the words, read the highlighted letters to get the answer to the riddle.

Answers, page 174.

What do people go to get, and end up with less than they started with?

	1	2	3	4
1				
2				
3				
4				

1 Place to wear your hat
2 "He flies through the air with the greatest of ___"
3 Biggest continent
4 Starting word for a letter

	1	2	3	4
1				
2				
3				
4				

1 Seafood similar to an oyster
2 Artificial bait for a fisherman
3 ___ and crafts
4 Untidy jumble or clutter

43

Check It Twice

Although these two pictures may seem identical, there are actually nine differences between them. When you find a difference, draw a straight line connecting the item in the top picture to its changed counterpart in the bottom picture. (You may want to use a ruler.) Each line you draw will cross out a letter. When you're done, the leftover letters, in order, will spell the answer to the riddle.

Answers, page 174.

What sport does Santa practice to keep in shape?

S P O C L A H E D V R A U G L N I T

What Not

In this quiz of your knowledge and intuition, one item doesn't belong in each of the groups. Can you guess which one?

Answers, page 174.

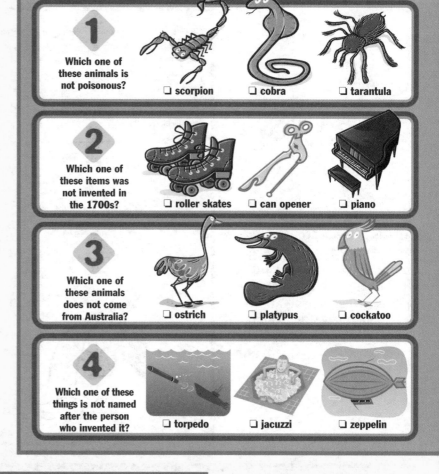

1 Which one of these animals is not poisonous?
❏ scorpion   ❏ cobra   ❏ tarantula

2 Which one of these items was not invented in the 1700s?
❏ roller skates   ❏ can opener   ❏ piano

3 Which one of these animals does not come from Australia?
❏ ostrich   ❏ platypus   ❏ cockatoo

4 Which one of these things is not named after the person who invented it?
❏ torpedo   ❏ jacuzzi   ❏ zeppelin

What does a wizard need if he wants to go skiing before winter arrives?

1 ⬊ Green things on trees
2 ⬈ Makes a sculpture out of wood
2 ⬊ Cardboard container for milk
3 ⬈ Fastener on a shirt
3 ⬊ Servant in a mansion
4 ⬈ Ice chest
4 ⬊ Used the stove
5 ⬈ Dipped cookies in milk
5 ⬊ Dimwits
6 ⬈ Seasonings like nutmeg and cinnamon
6 ⬊ Web spinner
7 ⬈ A firefighter might climb one
7 ⬊ Utensils for serving soup

Downhill Run

To find the answer to the riddle, use the clues to fill in the words in the spaces provided. Each word is split into two halves. One part goes with the word half above it, and the other part goes with the word half below it (except for the first and last halves). The arrow in each clue tells you in which direction your answer should go. When you're done, read the highlighted letters in order, from top to bottom, to get the answer to the riddle.

Answers, page 174.

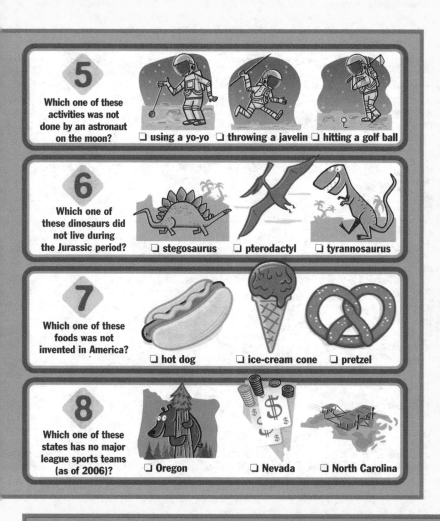

5 Which one of these activities was not done by an astronaut on the moon?

❏ using a yo-yo ❏ throwing a javelin ❏ hitting a golf ball

6 Which one of these dinosaurs did not live during the Jurassic period?

❏ stegosaurus ❏ pterodactyl ❏ tyrannosaurus

7 Which one of these foods was not invented in America?

❏ hot dog ❏ ice-cream cone ❏ pretzel

8 Which one of these states has no major league sports teams (as of 2006)?

❏ Oregon ❏ Nevada ❏ North Carolina

"You puny Earthlings have posed piddling riddles to each other since ancient times."

45

Knockouts

To solve this puzzle, first read the list of directions and cross out any pictures that apply. In each step, you will delete one, two, or three pictures. When you're done, four pictures will remain. Identify their names in order from top to bottom, left to right, to get the answer to the riddle.

Answers, page 174.

1. **Knock out any picture whose name is also the name of an animal.**
2. **Knock out any picture whose name begins and ends with the same letter.**
3. **Knock out any picture of an object that has strings.**
4. **Knock out any picture whose name sounds like a day of the week.**
5. **Knock out any two pictures whose names rhyme with each other.**
6. **Knock out any picture of an object that has a shell.**

What kind of person can pass and fail at the same time?

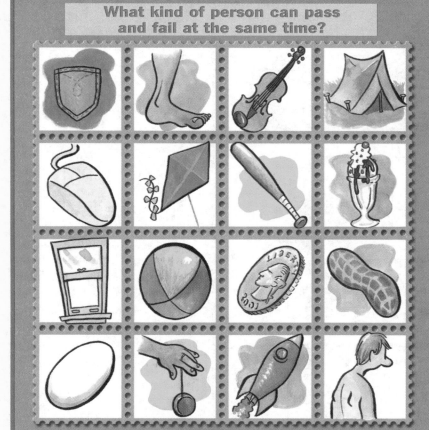

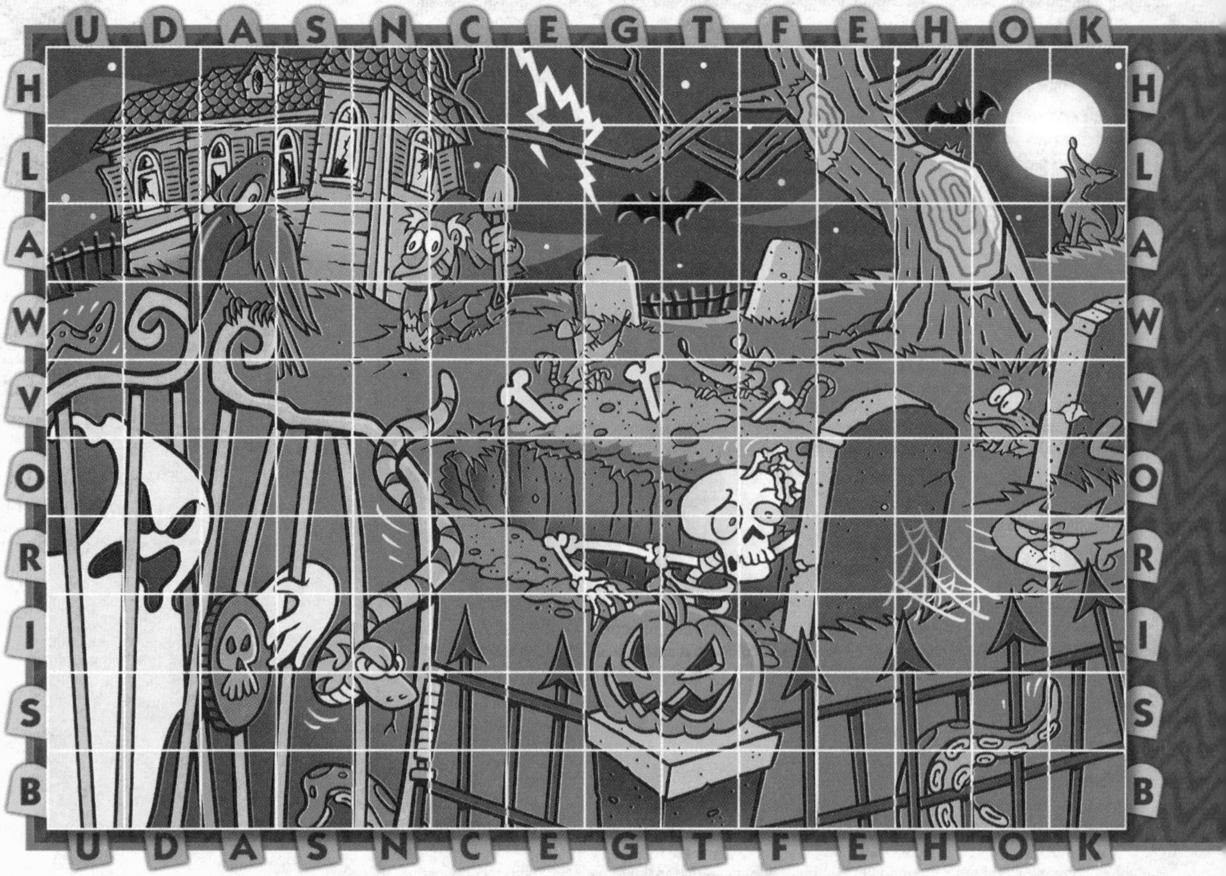

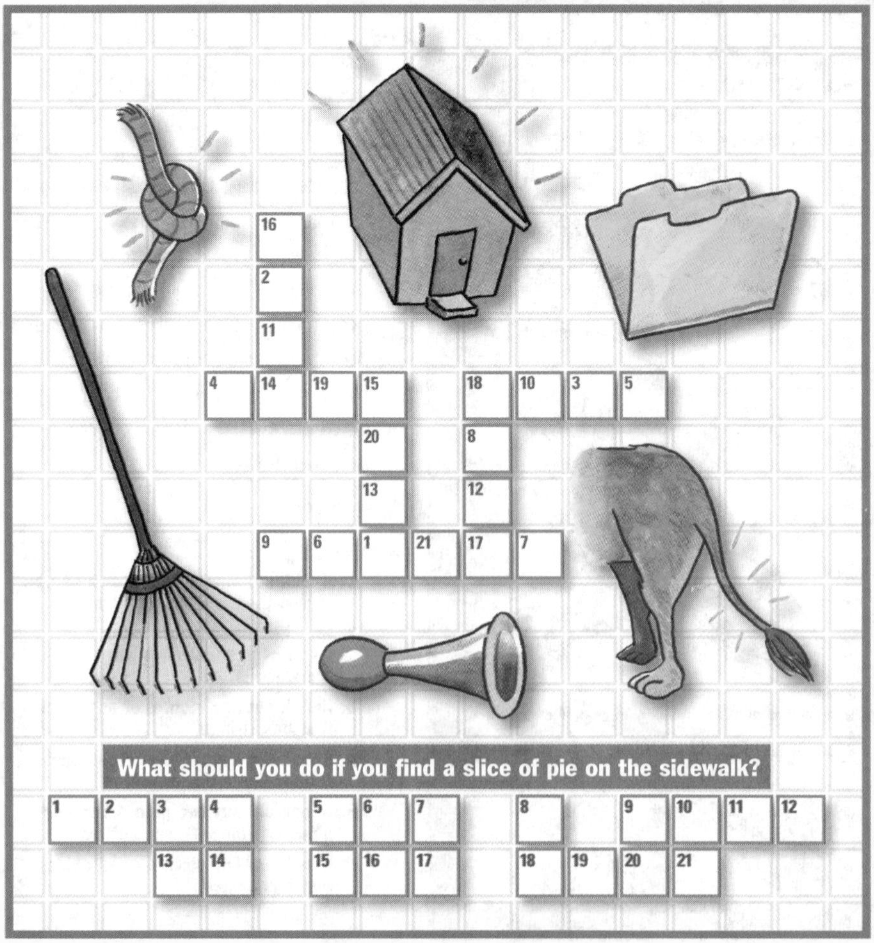

U D A S N C E G T F E H O K
H L A W V O R I S B
H L A W V O R I S B
U D A S N C E G T F E H O K

What should you do if you find a slice of pie on the sidewalk?

Find Dining

This puzzle has two parts. First, name the six pictures and figure out where to put the words in the crossword. Second, transfer the letters from the crossword to the numbered boxes at the bottom to get the answer to the riddle. Hint: Start by filling in the only six-letter word.

Answers, page 175.

Why couldn't the skeleton understand his tombstone?

I T

Scavenger Haunt

To get the answer to the riddle, look at the eight individual pieces and find them in the large picture. (Careful, some pieces have been rotated.) When you find a piece, write the letters showing where it came from—the row first (yellow stone) and the column second (orange stone). When you've found them all, those letters will spell out, in order, the answer to the riddle. The location of the first piece has been filled in for you.

Answers, page 174.

Hear and There

To find the answer to the riddle, draw a straight line from each picture on the left to the one on the right that is said to make the same noise. The pictures of the circular saw and the bee (both of which are said to buzz) have been connected to get you started. Each line you draw will cross out some letters. When you're finished, read the leftover letters in order, from top to bottom, to get the answer to the riddle.

Answers, page 175.

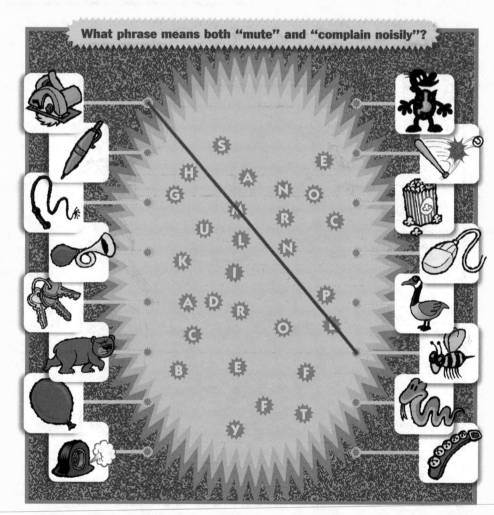

What phrase means both "mute" and "complain noisily"?

S H G A N E U K L R O I C A D P R B O E L F Y F T

Write Off the Bat

Fill in each row of boxes with the name of one of the objects shown here. One letter from each word has been placed to get you started. When you've filled every box, read down the two columns of shaded boxes to discover the answer to the riddle.

Answers, page 175.

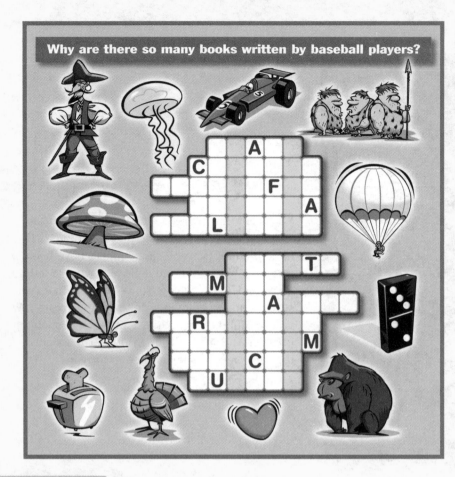

Why are there so many books written by baseball players?

48

How is a good detective like someone who sits on a new CD?

Riddle Middle

First identify each pair of pictures and write their names in the boxes. Each group of shaded boxes will spell out a word. When you're done, read these words in order to get the answer to the riddle.

Answers, page 175.

How did the explorer describe his compass after the needle fell off?

PLOIUSNETLGERASKS

No Way!

Although these two pictures may seem identical, there are actually seven differences between them. When you find a difference, draw a straight line connecting the item in the top picture to its changed counterpart in the bottom picture. (You may want to use a ruler.) Each line you draw will cross out a letter. When you're done, the leftover letters, in order, will spell the answer to the riddle.

Answers, page 175.

49

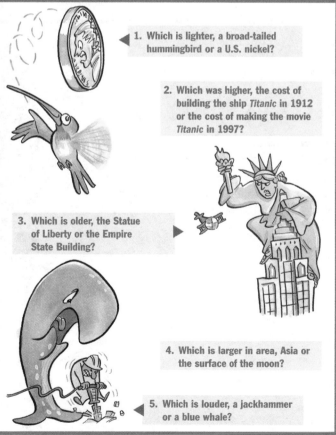

1. Which is lighter, a broad-tailed hummingbird or a U.S. nickel?

2. Which was higher, the cost of building the ship *Titanic* in 1912 or the cost of making the movie *Titanic* in 1997?

3. Which is older, the Statue of Liberty or the Empire State Building?

4. Which is larger in area, Asia or the surface of the moon?

5. Which is louder, a jackhammer or a blue whale?

Dare to Compare

See if you can pick which of the two items in each question is more ... whatever!

Answers, page 175.

1. The longest snake ever found was a python measuring 22 feet. Is that number ❏ high or ❏ low?

2. Dr. Seuss used only **104** different words to write *Green Eggs and Ham*. Is that number ❏ high or ❏ low?

3. If Jupiter were hollow, you could fit **310** Earths inside. Is that number ❏ high or ❏ low?

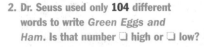

4. Walt Disney won more Oscars in his lifetime than anyone else, with **35**. Is that number ❏ high or ❏ low?

5. The alphabet used in the Hawaiian language has **20** letters. Is that number ❏ high or ❏ low?

7. Basketball player Wilt Chamberlain holds the record for points scored by one player in a single NBA game, with **62**. Is that number ❏ high or ❏ low?

6. In 1993, a man set a world record by staying on a tightrope for **36** days. Is that number ❏ high or ❏ low?

Sorry, Wrong Number

In each of these amazing statements, there's just one problem: the amazing part. Every time a number appears, it's actually wrong. Read each statement and decide whether you think that number is too high or too low.

Answers, page 175.

"Your Earthling 'question mark' may have come from the Latin word for 'question,' which was abbreviated to qo, with the Q over the o."

What keeps bolts from falling off a gingerbread house?

S D R O T U G L H A N O U T H S

How Sweet It Is

Although these two pictures may seem identical, there are actually seven differences between them. When you find a difference, draw a straight line connecting the item in the top picture to its changed counterpart in the bottom picture. (You may want to use a ruler.) Each line you draw will cross out a letter. When you're done, the leftover letters, in order, will spell the answer to the riddle.

Answers, page 175.

51

Now Hear Hiss

This puzzle has two parts. First, name the six pictures and figure out where to put the words in the crossword. Second, transfer the letters from the crossword to the numbered boxes at the bottom to get the answer to the riddle.

Answers, page 175.

Why can't a snake ever win an argument?

52

Why didn't Santa find any hot chocolate waiting for him on Christmas Eve?

Sweet Nothings

This puzzle has two parts. First, name the six pictures and figure out where to put the words in the crossword. Second, transfer the letters from the crossword to the numbered boxes at the bottom to get the answer to the riddle.

Answers, page 175.

Why did the kid regret winning the pie-eating contest at the county fair?

F I

Fair and Squares

To get the answer to the riddle, look at the 10 individual pieces and find them in the large picture. (Careful, some pieces have been rotated.) When you find a piece, write the letters showing where it came from—the column first (the purple banner) and the row second (the yellow banner). When you've found them all, those letters will spell out, in order, the answer to the riddle. The location of the first piece has been filled in for you.

Answers, page 176.

53

Ups and Downs

To find the answer to the riddle, use the clues to fill in the words in the spaces provided. Each word is split into two halves. One part goes with the word half above it, and the other part goes with the word half below it (except for the first and last halves). The arrow in each clue tells you in which direction your answer should go. When you're done, read the highlighted letters in order, from top to bottom, to get the answer to the riddle.

Answers, page 175.

What goes up when it's coming down?

1. ↘ Pail
2. ↗ Where the first "little piggy" went
2. ↘ Sculptures and counter-tops may be made of this
3. ↗ Where a horse lives
3. ↘ Booths in a public restroom
4. ↗ Tools for making holes
4. ↘ Person behind the wheel of a car
5. ↗ Animal that builds dams
5. ↘ Long-eared dog
6. ↗ A snarl in your hair
6. ↘ Large ship for carrying oil
7. ↗ Place to store your clothes at the gym
7. ↘ Find on a map

"The Sphinx in Egypt is a statue of a mythological monster who killed any puny Earthling who could not answer her riddle."

1 Which one of these animals never hibernates?

Earthworm

Porcupine

Frog

2 Which one of these sports is not part of the Winter Olympics?

Ice dancing

Snowboarding

Snowmobiling

5 Which statement about Alaska is not true?

Its state flag was designed by a 13-year-old

Its name means "Land of the Walrus"

It was bought from Russia for about $7 million

6 Which item was not found with a man who had been frozen in ice for 5,300 years?

Fur earmuffs

Grass cloak

Stone knife

54

Why don't witches travel while they're angry?

Which Is Witch?

Fill in each row of boxes with the name of one of the objects shown here. One letter from each word has been placed to get you started. When you've filled every box, read down the two columns of shaded boxes to discover the answer to the riddle.

Answers, page 176.

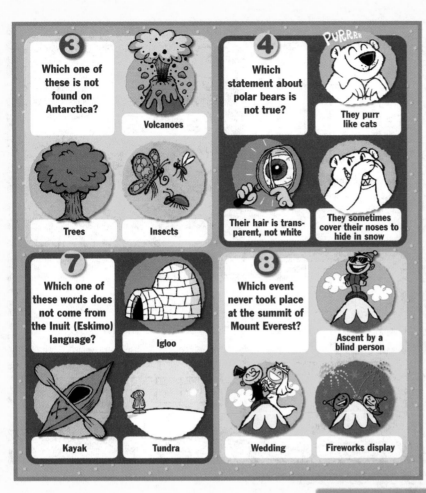

3
Which one of these is not found on Antarctica?

Volcanoes

Trees

Insects

4
Which statement about polar bears is not true?

PURRRR

They purr like cats

Their hair is transparent, not white

They sometimes cover their noses to hide in snow

7
Which one of these words does not come from the Inuit (Eskimo) language?

Igloo

Kayak

Tundra

8
Which event never took place at the summit of Mount Everest?

Ascent by a blind person

Wedding

Fireworks display

Cold Hard Facts

In this quiz of your cold-weather knowledge and guesswork, one item doesn't belong in each of the groups. Can you pick which one?

Answers, page 176.

Shooting Star

Although these two pictures may seem identical, there are actually seven differences between them. When you find a difference, draw a straight line connecting the item in the top picture to its changed counterpart in the bottom picture. (You may want to use a ruler.) Each line you draw will cross out a letter. When you're done, the leftover letters, in order, will spell the answer to the riddle.

Answers, page 176.

Where did the stuntman end up after his dangerous audition?

RIGONTSHLECANSTP

Holiday Notes

To solve the riddle, use the clues to fill in as many answer words as you can. The answers are the same both across and down, so enter each word in both directions to complete the puzzle. When you've filled in all the words, some letters will appear in colored boxes. Transfer those letters to the same colored boxes below the riddle to spell the riddle's answer.

Answers, page 176.

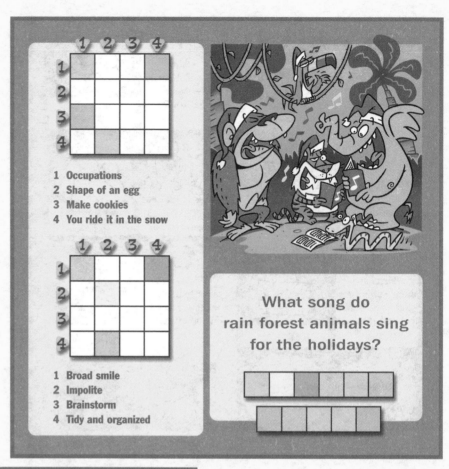

1 Occupations
2 Shape of an egg
3 Make cookies
4 You ride it in the snow

1 Broad smile
2 Impolite
3 Brainstorm
4 Tidy and organized

What song do rain forest animals sing for the holidays?

What word for a kind of baseball player becomes two pieces of clothing when you break it in two?

1
2
3
4
5
6
7

1 ↘ Precious metal sometimes used to make forks
2 ↗ Person who uses a razor
2 ↘ The sun casts one behind you
3 ↗ You can look through this to see outside
3 ↘ Coldest season
4 ↗ Person who swings at a baseball
4 ↘ Drum majorettes send them twirling into the air

5 ↗ These can be used to stir hot chocolate
5 ↘ You can use this to soak up a spill
6 ↗ Loose coins
6 ↘ Visual aids like graphs
7 ↗ Basketball games are played on these
7 ↘ You can cut this out to save money while shopping

Break It Up!

To find the answer to the riddle, use the clues to fill in the words in the spaces provided. Each word is split into two halves. One part goes with the word half above it, and the other part goes with the word half below it (except for the first and last halves). The arrow in each clue tells you in which direction your answer should go. When you're done, read the highlighted letters in order, from top to bottom, to get the answer to the riddle.

Answers, page 176.

Why didn't the twins enjoy their campout?

Double Cross

This puzzle has two parts. First, name the seven pictures and figure out where to put the words in the crossword. Second, transfer the letters from the crossword to the numbered boxes at the bottom to get the answer to the riddle.

Answers, page 176.

The Inside Story

To find the answer to the riddle, draw a straight line from each picture on the left to the picture on the right whose name contains the other picture's name inside it. The pictures of the ram and the frame have been connected to get you started. Each line you draw will cross out some letters. When you're finished, read the leftover letters in order, from top to bottom, to get the answer to the riddle.

Answers, page 177.

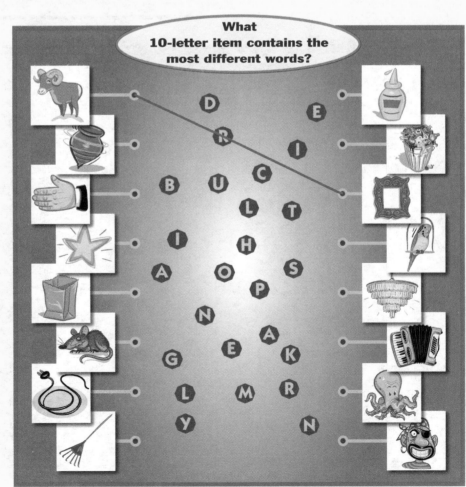

What 10-letter item contains the most different words?

Monster Match

This puzzle has two parts. First, name the six pictures and figure out where to put the words in the crossword. Second, transfer the letters from the crossword to the numbered boxes at the bottom to get the answer to the riddle.

Answers, page 177.

Why were Frankenstein's monster and the bride of Frankenstein so happy together?

58

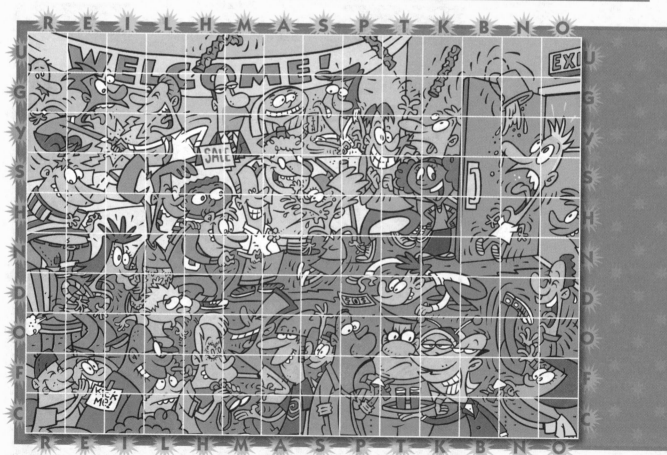

Double Space

Although these two pictures may seem identical, there are actually nine differences between them. When you find a difference, draw a straight line connecting the item in the top picture to its changed counterpart in the bottom picture. (You may want to use a ruler.) Each line you draw will cross out a letter. When you're done, the leftover letters, in order, will spell the answer to the riddle.

Answers, page 177.

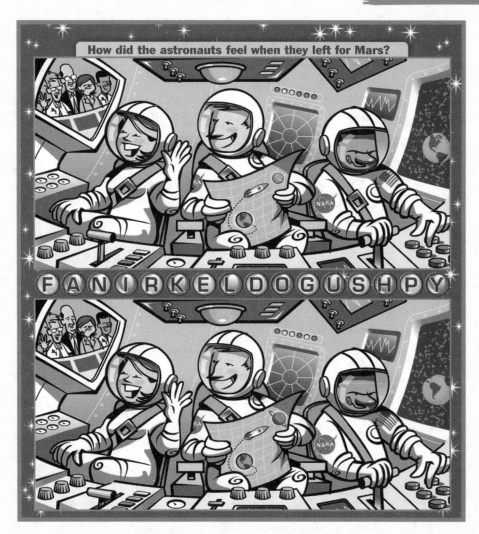

How did the astronauts feel when they left for Mars?

F A N I R K E L D O G U S H P Y

59

Why didn't the practical joke salesman sell funny perfumes?

H E

Jokers Wild

To get the answer to the riddle, look at the 10 individual pieces and find them in the large picture. (Careful, some pieces have been rotated.) When you find a piece, write the letters showing where it came from—the row first (green burst) and the column second (yellow burst). When you've found them all, those letters will spell out, in order, the answer to the riddle. The location of the first piece has been filled in for you.

Answers, page 177.

Follow these instructions carefully — and use a pencil with an eraser — and you may find a million-dollar treasure!

✣ If King Arthur's table was square, draw a square in box 3. If it was round, draw a circle in box 3.

✣ If the sun sets in the east, draw a capital E in box 5. If it doesn't set in the east, draw a backward capital E in box 5.

✣ If a flock of geese flies in a V shape, put a V in box 10. If a flock of geese flies in an S shape, put an S in box 10.

✣ If "What goes up must come down" is a common phrase, draw an exclamation point in box 7. If "What goes down must come up" is a common phrase, draw a smiley face in box 7.

✣ If Thanksgiving comes before Halloween in a calendar year, put a 4 in box 1. If Halloween comes before Thanksgiving in a calendar year, put a 5 in box 1.

✣ If a cello is bigger than a violin, draw a lowercase d in box 9. If a violin is bigger than a cello, draw a capital D in box 9.

✣ What letter can you insert somewhere in CANE to spell a form of transportation? If it's an O, draw an O in box 4. If it's an L, draw an L in box 4.

✣ If there are six days in a week that begin with a consonant, put a 6 in box 2. If there are seven days in a week that begin with a consonant, put a 7 in box 2.

✣ If more people are left-handed than right-handed, draw a capital L in box 8. If fewer people are left-handed than right-handed, draw a backward capital L in box 8.

✣ If — is a horizontal line, draw a — across the center of the letter in box 10. If | is a horizontal line, draw a | down the center of the letter in box 10.

✣ If this is the ninth instruction, erase the letter you've drawn in box 5. If this is not the ninth instruction, only remove the top bar from the letter in box 5.

✣ If you've drawn a 6 in box 2, draw another 6 in box 6. If you've drawn a 7 in box 2, draw another 7 in box 6.

When you've completed all the instructions, turn your answers upside down to find the treasure.

Treasure Jest

This mysterious note was found in a bottle. See what kind of fortune it leads you to.

Answers, page 177.

1 Repetition of sounds
2 Chocolate ___ cookie
3 Home for bees
4 Word to say before "sesame"

1 Wild pig
2 Shrek is one
3 An octopus has eight of these
4 Relaxation

What's the best feature of a hotel run by witches?

Witch You Were Here

To solve the riddle, use the clues to fill in as many answer words as you can. The answers are the same both across and down, so enter each word in both directions to complete the puzzle. When you've filled in all the words, some letters will appear in boxes with symbols. Transfer those letters to the boxes below the riddle with the same symbols to spell the riddle's answer.

Answers, page 177.

Night Shift

To find the answer to the riddle, use the clues to fill in the words in the spaces provided. Each word is split into two halves. One part goes with the word half above it, and the other part goes with the word half below it (except for the first and last halves). The arrow in each clue tells you in which direction your answer should go. When you're done, read the highlighted letters in order, from top to bottom, to get the answer to the riddle.

Answers, page 177.

If one brother oversleeps and one brother undersleeps, what do they need?

1 ✎ Person who asks for handouts
2 ✎ Mountain lion
2 ✎ You can clip it to save money at the supermarket
3 ✎ Sword, ray gun, or club
3 ✎ Less strong
4 ✎ Pen with a wide felt tip
4 ✎ Playing piece in a game of Chinese checkers
5 ✎ Suitable for being devoured
5 ✎ Lightbulb inventor
6 ✎ Rhyme and _____
6 ✎ Person enjoying a book
7 ✎ Item on a fire truck
7 ✎ Grown girls

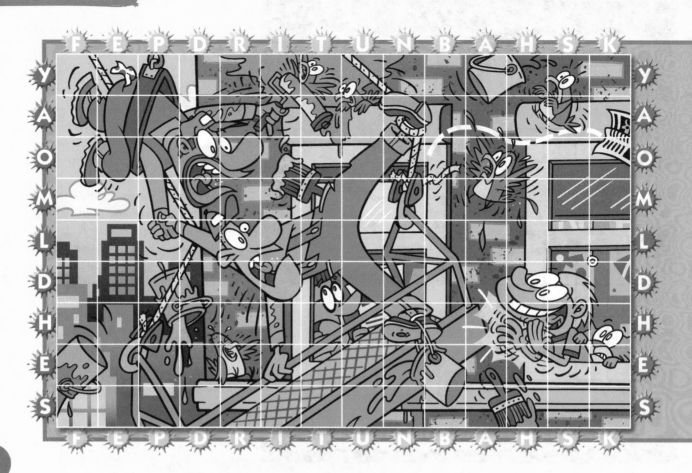

62

What is a rock band's favorite picnic food?

Tuning Out

To solve this puzzle, first read the list of directions and cross out any pictures that apply. In each step, you will delete one, two, or three pictures. When you're done, two pictures will remain. Identify their names in order from top to bottom to get the answer to the riddle.

Answers, page 177.

1. Knock out any picture whose name rhymes with **SING**.
2. Knock out any picture whose name becomes **BAND** if you change one letter.
3. Knock out any picture whose name has the word **EAR** somewhere in it.
4. Knock out any picture whose name is the same word as any of the other pictures.
5. Knock out any picture whose name consists of the five letters N, O, T, E, and S in any order.
6. Knock out any picture of something that has a **BOW**.

Why did the kid applaud for the tangled painters?

Flying Colors

To get the answer to the riddle, look at the 10 individual pieces and find them in the large picture. (Careful, some pieces have been rotated.) When you find a piece, write the letters showing where it came from—the column first (yellow splat) and the row second (green splat). When you've found them all, those letters will spell out, in order, the answer to the riddle. The location of the first piece has been filled in for you.

Answers, page 178.

For Starters

To find the answer to the riddle, draw a straight line from each picture on the left to the one on the right whose name starts with the sound of the entire first word. The pictures of the beak and the beacon have been connected to get you started. Each line you draw will cross out some letters. When you're finished, read the leftover letters in order, from top to bottom, to get the answer to the riddle.

Answers, page 178.

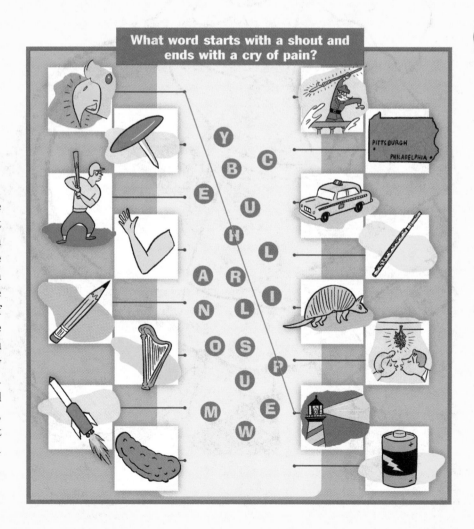

What word starts with a shout and ends with a cry of pain?

3

Alice in Wanderland

Mazes
with all kinds of
unexpected twists

Island Hopping

This poor castaway is stuck on the Puzzle Islands, where it's tough to find your way out. Start by choosing any of the items on the castaway's island (the palm tree doesn't count). Now find the exact same item somewhere else and jump to that island. Then choose another item on that new island and look for that same item somewhere else. Keep going until you get to the island with the boat at the bottom right . . . but look out for dead ends along the way!

Answers, page 178.

66

Wrap Stars

These two mummies didn't plan to stay in touch, but there's one strip of gauze here somewhere that connects them to each other. All the other pieces wind their way over and under each other but turn into "dead" ends. Can you find the only piece that makes the connection?

Answers, page 178.

Are We There Yet?

Sorry for the inconvenience, but you'll need to take a little detour. Can you find the correct path to the mall's side parking lot before you run out of gas?

Answers, page 178.

67

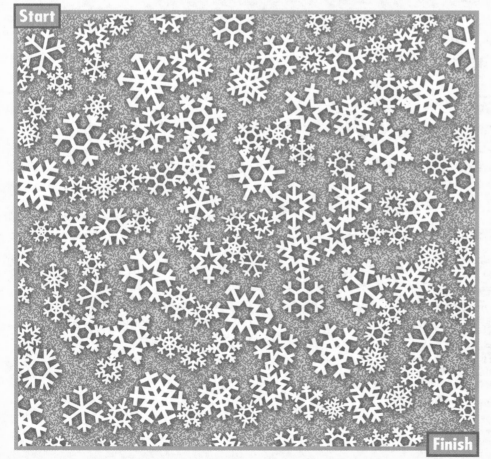

Dashing Through the Snow

Can you plow your way through the snow (staying only on the blue areas) from START to FINISH?

Answers, page 179.

Go With the Flow

Can you get from START to FINISH without getting burned?

Answers, page 179.

What Goes Around?

Start at the word "What" in the center, and find the path that leads to the exit at the bottom. If you take the correct path, the words you pass along the way will form a riddle. Can you solve it? Be careful—the wrong paths spell out nonsense questions that have no answer!

Answers, page 179.

"The inner ear is called the labyrinth because it is so very much like a maze!"

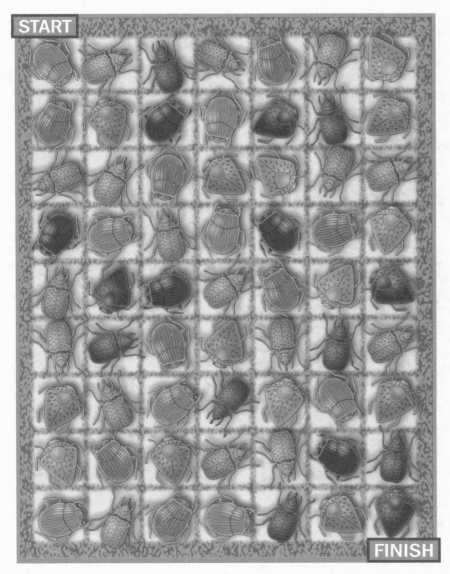

START

FINISH

Bug Out

Y ou'll have to creep and crawl your way through this batch of beetles to solve this maze. You may move left, right, up, or down (but not diagonally) to the next beetle only if it is either the same color or the same shape as the one you're on. Start on the round orange beetle at the upper left. From there, you may move either to the orange one next to it or the round one below it. Keep moving until you reach the beetle at the bottom right.

Answers, page 179.

70

Potion in Motion

Dr. Frankenstein's lab has become a maze of beakers, jars, and tubes. Here's an experiment: Can you find your way from Igor to the Mad Doctor's beaker following the path of the strange potion? Bonus puzzle: Find five skulls hidden in the picture!

Answers, page 179.

Flea Circuit

Ever wonder how a flea gets around? To solve this unusual maze, start by choosing a dog from the group of three at the top left. Now find the exact same dog in the exact same pose somewhere else and jump to that dog. Then choose another dog in that new group and look for an identical dog somewhere else. Keep going until you get to the group with the flea-free dog at the bottom right . . . but look out for dead ends along the way!

Answers, page 179.

The Long Run

Help this runner complete the marathon by taking him along one of the yellow pathways to the podium at the bottom. (No fair going around the outer edge!) When you're done, darken your path and hold the puzzle at arm's length to see how he did.

Answers, page 179.

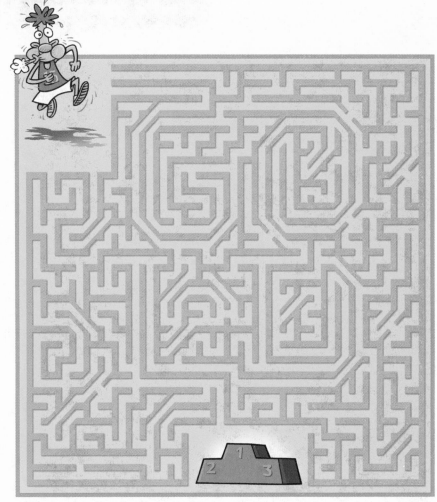

Chicken Out

Want to know why the chicken really crossed the road? To solve this maze! Starting from the chicken, can you cross the road and get to The Other Side without getting lost?

Answers, page 179.

72

Web Search

Can you get from the spider at the outside of this web to the fly at the center, traveling only along the strands of the web? Watch out for trapped flies—those are dead ends!

Answers, page 180.

Stick Around

D on't get stuck as you travel through this maze. You may move left, right, up, or down (but not diagonally) to the next stamp only if it has one of the same colors as the stamp you're on. Start on the yellow-and-red stamp at the upper left. From there, you may move either to the stamp with a red border next to it or the one with yellow continents below it. Keep moving until you reach the last stamp at the bottom right.

Answers, page 180.

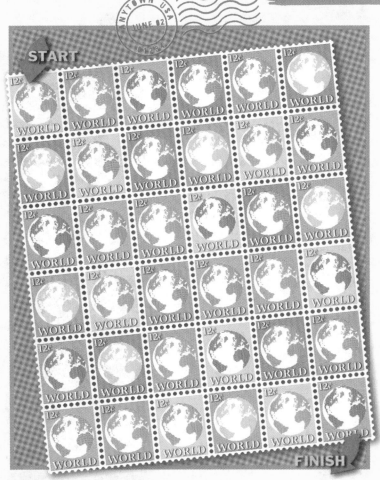

73

That's a Wrap!

Y ou'll be up to your neck in twists and turns as you find the only path from the knitter at the top to the boy at the bottom. Follow the paths as they wrap over and under each other.

Answers, page 180.

Garden Path

To solve this unusual butterfly maze, you'll have to do a little fluttering yourself. To start, choose any butterfly on the leaf at the upper left. Now find the exact same butterfly somewhere else and jump to its leaf. Then choose another butterfly on your new leaf and look for an identical butterfly somewhere else. Keep going until you get to the leaf at the bottom right . . . but look out for dead ends along the way!

Answers, page 180.

74

A Run of Luck

One of the clover patches in this maze is hiding a lucky four-leaf clover among the ordinary three-leaf clovers. But which patch is it? Start at the leprechaun and follow a continuous path till you get to one of the patches, adding and subtracting numbers along the way as you pass over them. If your total is 4 when you arrive at the patch, you've found the four-leaf clover. If your total is 3, go back to the beginning and see if you have better luck next time!

Answers, page 180.

Dig In!

No bones about it: This archaeological site is tough to get around. The archaeologist at the top left needs to get to his partner at the bottom right, but he has to walk around the dinosaur bones to get there. Which is the only path that will work?

Answers, page 180.

"Fancy that! Each year, hundreds of cornfields are plowed into mazes, many of which appear as pictures from the sky!"

Bee Lines

G et buzzy! See if you can make your way through the hive from START to FINISH.

Answers, page 180.

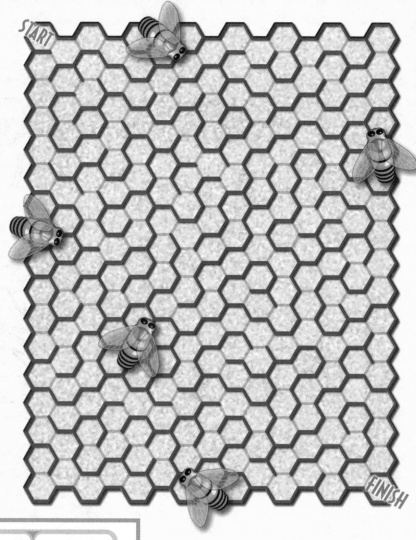

76

On the Word Path

E ach of the pictures in this maze represents one word. Move from one picture to the next—up, down, left, or right— only if the two words pictured can be combined, in order, to form a complete word or phrase. Start with the tooth at the upper left. You can move either to the brush below it, making the word "toothbrush," or to the pick to its right, making "toothpick." But beware of paths that lead nowhere! Only one path will get you all the way to the finish.

Answers, page 180.

Dead End

See if you can find your way from the bottom of the gate into the FINISH letters by traveling between the iron bars.

Answers, page 181.

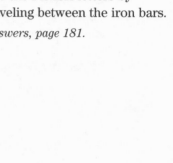

Clearance Sail

The poor guy on the raft has finally made it back to civilization, but he's not out of the water yet. Can you help him find the only unbroken path of water to the open spot at the dock? He cannot raft under obstacles or pass through areas where the water is not visible.

Answers, page 181.

START

Hold Your Tongue!

Can you get the dragonfly from START to FINISH without becoming lunch for a frog? To do it, you'll have to travel over the water between lily pads without passing right in front of any frog. No flying off the edges of the pond!

Answers, page 181.

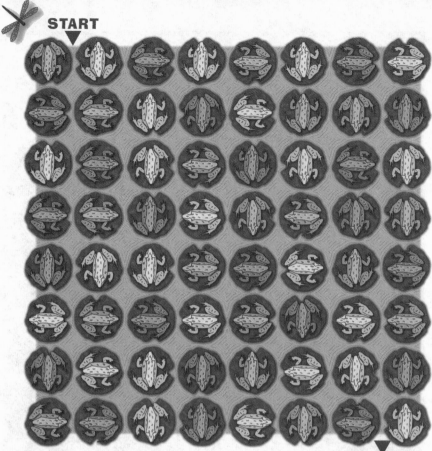

FINISH

78

Don't Go There

For this backward maze, the object is to NOT get to the finish! Begin in the START area and try to find the only path that winds up in a dead end. If you make it to FINISH, too bad—you'll have to go back and start all over.

Answers, page 181.

Floor Plan

Going up! Going down! Going crazy! In this maze, the elevator buttons tell you exactly where each elevator can take you. Start at the bottom left elevator, which takes you up one floor. When you get out, transfer to the only other elevator in that section. You'll then have to decide if you want to go up two floors or down one. Continue riding and transferring until you get to the party at the top right. Remember, you cannot walk through walls or enter any elevator without buttons.

Answers, page 181.

4

The Wordman of Alcatraz

Wordplay puzzles
for anyone
with a long spell
in the pen

Give Me a C! Give Me a D!

Sure, CDs have holes in the middle, but this is ridiculous. All of the words in this puzzle start with C and end with D, but the other letters are missing. Use the clues to fill them in.

Answers, page 181.

ACROSS

4 Small closet over a kitchen counter

5 Cape ___ is a popular Massachusetts vacation spot

8 Three or more notes played at one time

9 Person who is chicken

11 Creamy donut filling

12 Ohio city where the Indians play

DOWN

1 His arrows might make you fall in love

2 White puff in the sky

3 The kind of puzzle this is

5 Something you get in the mail on your birthday

6 Electrical wire that ends in a plug

7 TV show about three young witches

10 Brand of adhesive bandages

82

In the O Zone

Look around—and around—at this O-shaped grid and you'll find 30 words, reading left, right, up, down, and diagonally, that have the letter O as their only vowel. When you've found them all, read the leftover letters from left to right, starting at the top row, to get a bonus message. Now go on!

Answers, page 181.

```
        T P O N D W
      O R R O Z R O O P   P
    N S C H O O L R O O M   O
  N T C C H W J T O L C X B   H
  H O N F S S K O O B K O O   C
R O O O S O       M M B C T   F
S P O O N         O N O D O   O
O S R P O         T R L O O   O
L C K B W         O O R T R   R
O O B C B         G C O O L
T T S O O B         F O P B M W
C O L O R O O D O T R O O   D
H O N T M N O T Z W T P O G
O N S G B O H O T D O G
O G O P O O O F L O
  O F F X M F
```

BOOM BOX	DOOR-TO-DOOR	POLO	SNOW BOOTS
BOOST	FLOOD	PONCHO	SOLO
COCOON	HOBO	POPCORN BOX	SPOON
COLOR	HOPSCOTCH	POT OF GOLD	SWOOP
CONGO	HOT DOG	ROBOT	TOMORROW
COOKBOOK	MOON ROCK	ROOF	WOOL
COOL	NOON	SCHOOLROOM	ZOOM
CROSSWORD			ZORRO

| C | A | M | P |

A little bit wet

Place where the garbage trucks go

Chunk in your oatmeal

Walk with a hurt foot

It looks like a green lemon

Smallest U.S. coin

Jackknife or half-gainer

Highest number you can count on one hand

| F | I | R | E |

Hot Stuff

Can you change the word "camp" into "fire" one letter at a time? Use each clue to fill in a word that is only one letter different from the word before it. If you get stuck, try solving from the bottom up.

Answers, page 181.

83

Tag Team

Who's getting which gift this year? To find out, fill in the same letters in the same order on both lines of each gift tag. The first line will tell you who the present is for, and the second line will tell you the name of the present, which is shown beneath the tree. (Not every object will be used.) One tag has been filled in to get you started.

Answers, page 181.

Letter Openers

In this post office, letters are always bundled in groups of three. In fact, there are 12 things going on here that can each be described with a three-word phrase in which every word starts with the same letter. For example, the fellow behind the counter is a "Scarecrow Selling Stamps." Can you identify the 11 other three-word phrases? No letter is used to start more than one phrase.

Answers, page 182.

It's what the chicken crossed

Sound made by a lion or tiger

Back end of a bus or a person

Animal that likes honey

A band's drummer keeps this

Clean and tidy

Spellbound

Just how does a witch turn a "toad" into a "newt"? In this case, it happens one letter at a time! Use each clue to fill in a word that is only one letter different from the word before it. If you get stuck, try solving from the bottom up.

Answers, page 182.

Hawaiian Tour

loha! Hidden in this grid, reading left, right, up, down, and diagonally, are the 20 Hawaii-related things listed here. When you've found them all, read the left-over letters from left to right, starting at the top row, to get a cool fact. Pomaika`i! (That means "good luck!")

Answers, page 182.

```
P I N E A P P L E U K I
H U H L L E O E U L U E
U A O C G N I L I A S T
L H N T A A U A M L U O
A E O C O C O N U T R U
P A L M T R E E L C Y R
M O U E E A A N H S L I
V E L A L G N I F R U S
P L U I N U D G F L H T
G R A S S S K I R T A S
E A I V N H A U E W O A
I S D N A L S I I L A N
```

ALOHA	LEI	PINEAPPLE
COCONUT	LUAU	SAILING
GRASS SKIRT	MAUI	SUGARCANE
HONOLULU	OAHU	SURFING
HULA	ORCHIDS	TOURISTS
ISLANDS	PALM TREE	UKULELE
LAVA		VOLCANO

Chain of Command

By carrying letters down from one set of blanks to the next, you can get the names of 10 presidents. The colored paths show you which letters move down, but you'll have to fill in the remaining letters yourself. Colors are used for different letters in different parts of the puzzle. So, for example, even though a blue line connects the M in ADAMS to an M in the next name, blue may stand for other letters elsewhere.

Answers, page 182.

86

BUTTERFLY   FLYPAPER   HORSEFLY

DRAGONFLY   FLYSPECK   HOUSEFLY

FIREFLY   FLYSWATTER   POP FLY

FLY BALL   FRUIT FLY   SAND FLY

FLYING CARPET   GADFLY   STUNT FLYING

FLYING SAUCER   GO FLY A KITE   VENUS FLYTRAP

Catching Flies

What's the buzz? In this puzzle, it's that every place the letters F-L-Y appear together in the 18 words listed here, they've been replaced with a picture of a fly. For example, the word "flypaper" can be found in the grid as PAPER. The words are hidden reading left, right, up, down, and diagonally. When you've found them all, read the leftover letters from left to right, starting at the top row, to get a bonus message.

Answers, page 182.

Peter and Tippi had sharply different tastes in music. Peter liked to sit around in the tub and listen to jazz, while Tippi really responded to rock concerts.

One night, Tippi told Peter that she was planning on going to see her favorite band, even though she'd heard rumors that the concert was sold out. Her plan was to pack a zoom lens and a camera and blend in with all the paparazzi there.

"You think they're so disorganized, they let in every shutterbug left and right?" Peter asked.

Tippi said, "When I turn the charm on I can get past anyone."

"But tonight's ravioli night," Peter whined. "Would you really cancel long-standing plans?"

"Absolutely!" she replied, and left.

Before long, Tippi returned and threw the biggest tantrum Peter had ever seen. The police had given Tippi an order to go home for violating the law. Peter smiled as he said, "Will you feel better if I fetch you some cold ravioli?"

"In"strumental

The names of 18 musical instruments are hidden in this story. Some of them can be found completely within a word ("harp" is hidden in "sharply"), and some go across two or more words ("sitar" is hidden in "sit around"). Finding 10 is good, spotting 15 is excellent, and if you get all 18, you're a real musical pro.

Answers, page 182.

Odd Balls

You'll need to be on the ball for this puzzle, because each of the items being juggled represents a word or phrase that can end with "ball." For example, a can of paint would lead to the word PAINTBALL. How many of these can you figure out?

Answers, page 182.

Drawing Blanks

Every clue in this crossword puzzle is an illustration of the answer word. Place each word in the grid using the corresponding numbers. When you're done, read the highlighted letters from left to right, starting at the top row, to spell a bonus phrase.

Answers, page 182.

All Wet

Each of these eight words can follow "water" to form a familiar word or phrase, such as "waterproof"—but the words have been distorted by placing them underwater. Can you mentally towel them off and figure out each word?

Answers, page 182.

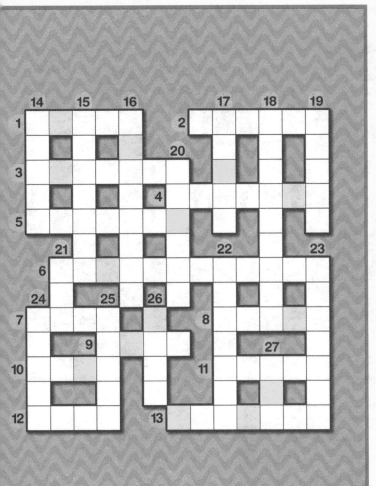

"Some French guy wrote an entire book without using a single E ... and another guy <u>translated it into English</u>, also without a single E!"

Treat or Trick?

C an you search this grid of letters and find the 25 treats listed here? No, you can't! That's because the trick is that only 20 of these treats are actually hidden in the grid. The words read left, right, up, down, and diagonally. When you've found the 20 treats, the leftover letters, read in order from left to right, starting at the top row, will spell a riddle. The first letter of each of the unfound treat words, in order, will spell the riddle's answer.

Answers, page 182.

```
E M A G O E D I V W S H O I K
Y S A L I W V A S Y G P Y P O
D S D K F U D G E T H U I E O
N P O P C O R N I C L Z M H B
A O N E O A O R R W Z Z I N C
C N U E C M R K F A I L N H I
A A T L O M A G I C S E T L M
O W K E A E N G A T M Y O Y O
E S T E K C I T T R E C N O C
```

CAKE
CANDY
CHIPS
COCOA
COMIC BOOK
CONCERT TICKET
COOKIE
DONUT
DVD
FRIES
FUDGE
GLOW STICK
GUM

HOT DOG
KITE
MAGIC SET
MONEY
ORANGE
PIZZA
POPCORN
PUZZLE
SUNDAE
TRADING CARDS
VIDEO GAME
YO-YO

Board Game

Each surfboard here illustrates a word that can be placed before "board" to make a new word. For example, a surfboard that showed a supermarket checker would be a CHECKERBOARD. How many of these can you figure out?

Answers, page 182.

Laugh Tracks

The 34 words listed here will fit into these boxes so that they all interlock like a crossword puzzle. All the words have the letter pair HA in them, which is given in the grid, but the other letters are missing. By using the lengths of the words and the places where they cross as a guide, can you put them all in the correct spots?

Answers, page 182.

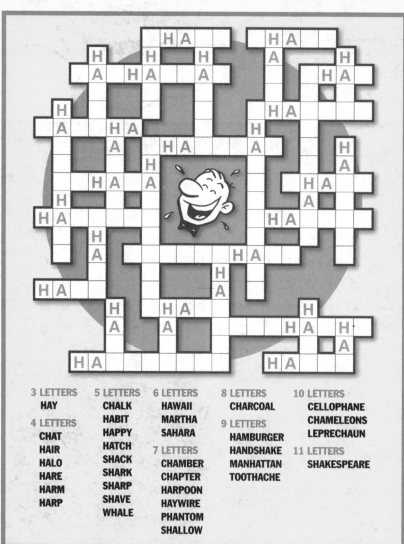

3 LETTERS	5 LETTERS	6 LETTERS	8 LETTERS	10 LETTERS
HAY	CHALK	HAWAII	CHARCOAL	CELLOPHANE
	HABIT	MARTHA		CHAMELEONS
4 LETTERS	HAPPY	SAHARA	9 LETTERS	LEPRECHAUN
CHAT	HATCH		HAMBURGER	
HAIR	SHACK	7 LETTERS	HANDSHAKE	11 LETTERS
HALO	SHARK	CHAMBER	MANHATTAN	SHAKESPEARE
HARE	SHARP	CHAPTER	TOOTHACHE	
HARM	SHAVE	HARPOON		
HARP	WHALE	HAYWIRE		
		PHANTOM		
		SHALLOW		

90

1 A apes B brake C crayons

2 A ats B build C castle

3 A_____ B_____ C_____

4 A angles B bake C cookes

5 A_____ B_____ C_____

6 A astonats B ath C ats

Easy as ABC

Each of these scenes can be described with a phrase whose first letters are ABC, such as Aardvarks Burning Candles. Can you identify all six ABC pictures?

Answers, page 182.

91

Big Deal

If you play your cards right, you'll find the 24 card-related things listed here, which are hidden in this grid reading left, right, up, down, and diagonally. When you've found them all, read the leftover letters from left to right, starting at the top row, to get a cool fact.

Answers, page 183.

ACE	GO FISH	QUEEN
CLUBS	HAND	RUMMY
CRAZY EIGHTS	HEARTS	SCORE
CUT	JACK	SHUFFLE
DEALER	JOKER	SOLITAIRE
DECK	KING	SPADES
DIAMONDS	PAIR	WAR
GAME	PILE	WILD CARD

Small Change

Each of these scenes can be described with a two-word phrase in which both words are the same except for one changed letter. For example, a drawing of a wall decoration showing Hogwarts School's most famous wizard would be a "Potter poster." Can you figure out the names of all eight pictures?

Answers, page 183.

Brain Storm

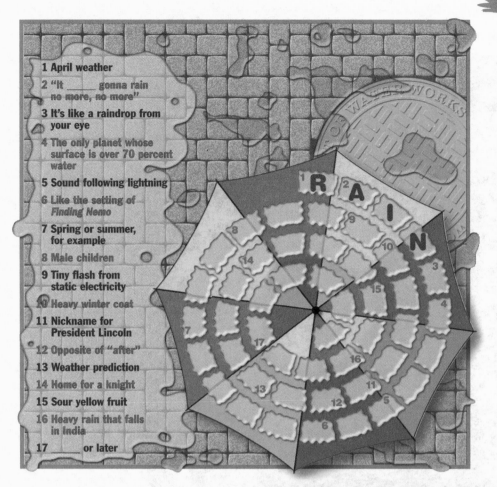

1 April weather

2 "It _____ gonna rain no more, no more"

3 It's like a raindrop from your eye

4 The only planet whose surface is over 70 percent water

5 Sound following lightning

6 Like the setting of *Finding Nemo*

7 Spring or summer, for example

8 Male children

9 Tiny flash from static electricity

10 Heavy winter coat

11 Nickname for President Lincoln

12 Opposite of "after"

13 Weather prediction

14 Home for a knight

15 Sour yellow fruit

16 Heavy rain that falls in India

17 _____ or later

Words go into this grid, one letter per space, starting with the first word, RAIN, and traveling inward around the spiral. Each new word starts in the box with the clue number, but then continues past the next number because each word overlaps the one before it. For example, Word 2 starts in the box numbered 2 and begins with the letters AIN. Use the letters from one answer to help solve the next one.

Answers, page 183.

93

Outback Pack

G'day, mate! This grid contains 22 words related to Australia (see the list Down Under the grid), reading left, right, up, down, and diagonally. When you've found them all, read the leftover letters from left to right, starting at the top row, to get a cool fact.

Answers, page 183.

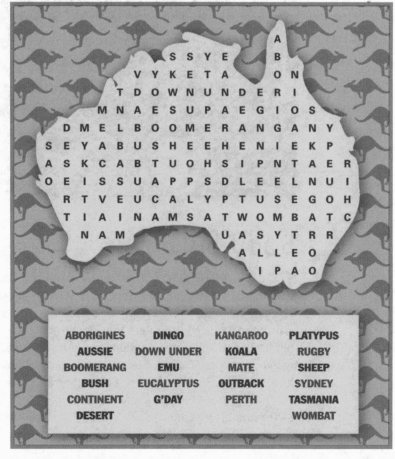

ABORIGINES	**DINGO**	**KANGAROO**	**PLATYPUS**
AUSSIE	**DOWN UNDER**	**KOALA**	**RUGBY**
BOOMERANG	**EMU**	**MATE**	**SHEEP**
BUSH	**EUCALYPTUS**	**OUTBACK**	**SYDNEY**
CONTINENT	**G'DAY**	**PERTH**	**TASMANIA**
DESERT			**WOMBAT**

94

Body Building

It may not look like Dr. Frankenstein has the body parts he needs, but they're all right here in his lab. Examine the body parts on his list and, for each part, search the picture for an item that either is known by that body part's name or contains something known by that body part's name. For example, the table on the left has LEGS. How many of the other parts can you find? (Ignore the parts that already belong to the doctor and his assistant.)

Answers, page 183.

Boxing Match

Fill in each row of boxes with the name of one of the objects shown here. One letter from each word has been placed to get you started. When you've filled every box, three pictures will remain unused. Read down the two columns of shaded boxes to discover a phrase that applies to the names of those three pictures.

Answers, page 183.

Shore Enough

Can you change the word "sand" into "dune" one letter at a time? Use each clue to fill in a word that is only one letter different from the word before it. If you get stuck, try solving from the bottom up.

Answers, page 183.

SAND

Harry Potter's magical stick

It makes the leaves rustle

Where a person's thoughts come from

Place to dig for coal

You might use a ruler to draw this

Last name of Superman's girlfriend

First name of Tarzan's girlfriend

Month in which summer starts

DUNE

Double Headers

Look twice! Hidden in this grid are the 12 pairs of words listed here that are spelled the same except for their first letter. For example, __ ONKEY and __ ONKEY are hidden in the grid as DONKEY and MONKEY. (None of the completed words are names.) The words are hidden reading left, right, up, down, and diagonally. When you've found them all, read the leftover letters from left to right, starting at the top row, to get a bonus message.

Answers, page 183.

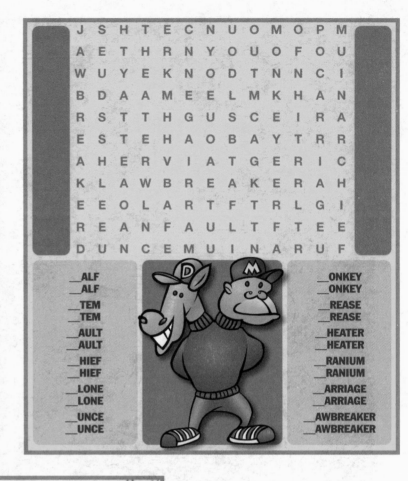

```
J S H T E C N U O M O P M
A E T H R N Y O U O F O U
W U Y E K N O D T N N C I
B D A A M E E L M K H A N
R S T T H G U S C E I R A
E S T E H A O B A Y T R R
A H E R V I A T G E R I C
K L A W B R E A K E R A H
E E O L A R T F T R L G I
R E A N F A U L T F T E E
D U N C E M U I N A R U F
```

__ALF	__ONKEY
__ALF	__ONKEY
__TEM	__REASE
__TEM	__REASE
__AULT	__HEATER
__AULT	__HEATER
__HIEF	__RANIUM
__HIEF	__RANIUM
__LONE	__ARRIAGE
__LONE	__ARRIAGE
__UNCE	__AWBREAKER
__UNCE	__AWBREAKER

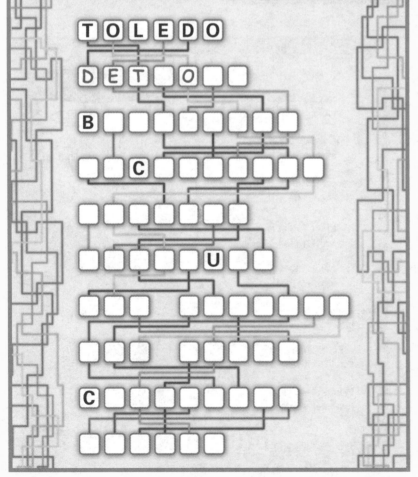

City Lines

By carrying letters down from one set of blanks to the next, you can get the names of 10 U.S. cities. The colored paths show you which letters move down, but you'll have to fill in the remaining letters yourself. Colors are used for different letters in different parts of the puzzle. So, for example, even though a purple line connects the D in TOLEDO to a D in the next city, purple may stand for other letters elsewhere.

Answers, page 183.

Cold Spell

The letters that make up these snowflakes come from "snow" words—words that can follow "snow" to form familiar words or phrases. The letters are scrambled, and some of them are even upside down. In addition, each set of letters appears six times. For example, Snowflake 1 contains the letters E, S, O, S, and H, and the answer is SHOES (as in "snowshoes"). Can you figure out what "snow" word appears in each snowflake?

Answers, page 183.

97

Pinwheel

Each of the pictures here can be identified with a four-letter word. Once you have each word, write it in the grid in the direction shown by its arrow, starting at the outside and moving in toward the center in an arc. One answer has been filled in to get you started.

Answers, page 183.

Get Packing

Can you turn "snow" into a "ball" one letter at a time? Use each clue to fill in a word that is only one letter different from the word before it. If you get stuck, try solving from the bottom up.

Answers, page 184.

S	N	O	W

Moving like a snail

It clears the streets of snow

The main story told in a book

Splotch of ink

Footwear for a snowy day

Canoe or kayak

"Don't ___ around the bush"

One way to hold your pants up

Inventor of the telephone

B	A	L	L

Same Hear!

The bad news is that the 25 words listed here *cannot* be found in this grid of letters. The good news is that you will be able to find a *homophone* of each word in the grid, reading left, right, up, down, or diagonally. (Homophones are words that sound the same but are spelled differently, such as WAIST and WASTE.) When you've found them all, read the leftover letters from left to right, starting at the top row, to get a bonus message.

Answers, page 184.

```
R R O L L D E W O L L A R
E E I S L H S E W O O D E
S A C R W T I I E A A C H
S M O E H E H G U O R H T
O W L R I B E H H U S N A
R N O S O P A T I E N C E
G N N R E S W S E W R S W
E M E I D U E S F L O U R
T D L O B M Y S N H U T N
```

ALOUD _____   PEACE _____   SUITE _____   WAIT _____
BOARD _____   ROLE _____   SUN _____   WHETHER _____
CREWS _____   SALE _____   THREW _____   WHIRLED _____
CYMBAL _____   SOARED _____   THROWN _____   WORN _____
FLOWER _____   SOME _____   TOE _____   WOULD _____
GROCER _____
HIRE _____
HOES _____
KERNEL _____
PATIENTS _____

98

99

Scene of the Rhyme

This scene contains six sets of three items that rhyme with each other. For example, if you spotted a BOULDER, you might also find a SHOULDER and a FOLDER. All the rhyming words have two syllables. Can you find all six sets?

Answers, page 183.

Veg Out

The blank in each sentence here can be filled in with the name of a vegetable—shown in the picture—that completes the sentence in a punny way. For example, the answer to the first sentence is "beans" (a pun on "beings"). How many will you get? Beets us!

Answers, page 184.

1. Dogs must think human _____ are pretty strange, since they throw their delicious bones in the garbage.

2. My parents talk so much when I watch TV that I have to _____ the volume to full blast.

3. I thought Mom would be upset that I came home late, but she really didn't seem to _____ all.

4. Whenever I get a present, I can't wait to rip off the wrapping _____ and see what's inside.

5. We wanted to eat dessert first, but our mom wouldn't _____.

6. It seems like whenever I get close to finishing a jigsaw puzzle, I find that there's one _____ missing.

7. We took a few roses from our neighbor's garden for Grandma's birthday because it was too late to _____ shop.

8. At the end of her mushy letter, Jennifer _____ and seven X's.

100

Open and Shut Case

The 21 things listed here will fit into these boxes so that the words all interlock like a crossword puzzle. But everywhere the letters L-O-C-K appear together in the words, they have been replaced in the grid with a picture of a lock, and everywhere the letters K-E-Y appear together, they have been replaced with a picture of a key. By using the lengths of the words and the places where they cross as a key to solving, can you get a lock on where everything belongs? (Ignore spaces and punctuation.)

Answers, page 184.

KEY RING
KEY WEST
LOW-KEY
MALARKEY
MICKEY MOUSE
ALARM CLOCK
BLACK EYED PEAS
MONKEY WRENCH
OARLOCKS
BLOCKADE
OKEY-DOKEY
CLOCKWISE
PADLOCK
CRIKEY!
SHERLOCK HOLMES
DONKEYS
SMOKEY BEAR
GOLDILOCKS
STUMBLING BLOCK
HEMLOCK
WARLOCK

```
B T F R E M M A H K C A J H E
O B O L E T E J L U E R W H L
O A G L Z R O O S T E R O L R
M U H E E A D I T H S N I W E
B M O U E F I R E W O R K S D
O C R G N F A H U N D U L O N
X U N D S I R E N M E R T T U
H O A N N C B A B Y S A P L H
G A N E R O C K C O N C E R T
```

BABY	JACKHAMMER
BOOM BOX	JET
BUGLE	ROCK CONCERT
CANNON	ROOSTER
CROWD	SHOUT
DRILL	SIREN
DRUMS	SNEEZE
FIREWORKS	THUNDER
FOGHORN	TRAFFIC
GONG	TRAIN

Keep It Down!

Can you hear us? This grid contains—we *said*, this grid contains the 20 noisy things listed here! They're hidden reading left, right, up, down, and diagonally! When you've found them all, read the leftover letters from left to right, starting at the top row, to get a cool fact! That's A COOL FACT!

Answers, page 184.

101

Crying Wolf

Can you change the word "full" into "moon" one letter at a time? Use each clue to fill in a word that is only one letter different from the word before it. If you get stuck, try solving from the bottom up.

Answers, page 184.

FULL

The season that Halloween is in

Big party that Cinderella went to

It's rung by the Hunchback of Notre Dame

A Batman costume includes a utility ___

Frankenstein's monster has one on each side of his neck

Pirate ship, for example

Alligator-filled trench around a castle

Pained cry from a ghost

MOON

102

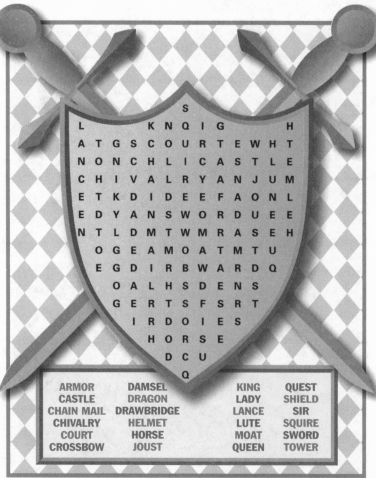

Knight Watch

Welcome, gentle folk, to a Search of Words on all things Medieval. Hidden in yonder grid are 24 words concerning the Legends of the Knights, which you must seek in the directions left, right, up, down, and diagonal. When you have completed your Quest, read the letters yet remaining from left to right, starting at the top row, for a Humorous Pronouncement.

Answers, page 184.

ARMOR	DAMSEL	KING	QUEST
CASTLE	DRAGON	LADY	SHIELD
CHAIN MAIL	DRAWBRIDGE	LANCE	SIR
CHIVALRY	HELMET	LUTE	SQUIRE
COURT	HORSE	MOAT	SWORD
CROSSBOW	JOUST	QUEEN	TOWER

Is Everything OK?

There are 13 things here that can be described by using the initials O.K. For example, that boat in the center of the picture is an "oily kayak." If you can find the other 12 things, that's A-OK!

Answers, page 184.

What in the World?

What country did each of these souvenirs come from? To find out, fill in the same letters in the same order on both lines of each tag. The first line will tell you the name of the country, and the second line will tell you the name of one of the souvenirs shown below the tags. One tag has been filled in to get you started.

Answers, page 184.

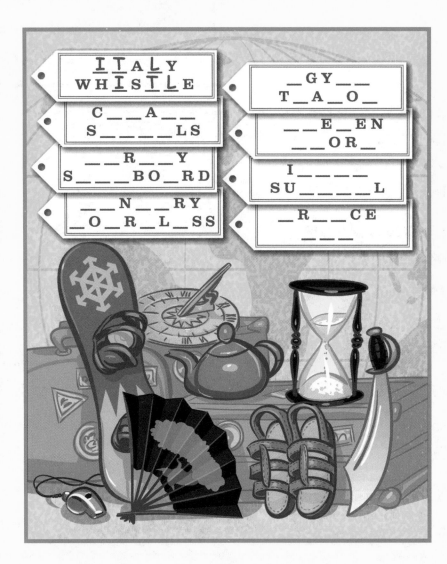

ITALY
WHISTLE

C _ _ A _ _
S _ _ _ _ _ LS

_ _ R _ _ Y
S _ _ _ BO _ RD

_ _ N _ _ RY
_ O _ R L _ SS

_ GY _ _ _
T _ A _ O _

_ _ E _ EN
_ _ OR _

I _ _ _ _ _
SU _ _ _ _ _ L

_ R _ _ CE
_ _ _

Sound Tracks

Can you change a "solo" into a "duet" one letter at a time? Use each clue to fill in a word that is only one letter different from the word before it. If you get stuck, try solving from the bottom up.

Answers, page 184.

SOLO

Tall, round structure next to a barn

Smooth as ___

Place to wash your hands and face

Red plus white makes this color

A guitar player may use this to pluck strings

Black disk used in ice hockey

"Lower your head!"

Twilight

Stuff that settles on shelves

DUET

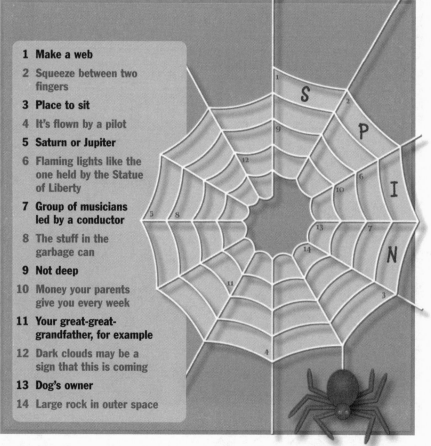

1 **Make a web**

2 **Squeeze between two fingers**

3 **Place to sit**

4 **It's flown by a pilot**

5 **Saturn or Jupiter**

6 **Flaming lights like the one held by the Statue of Liberty**

7 **Group of musicians led by a conductor**

8 **The stuff in the garbage can**

9 **Not deep**

10 **Money your parents give you every week**

11 **Your great-great-grandfather, for example**

12 **Dark clouds may be a sign that this is coming**

13 **Dog's owner**

14 **Large rock in outer space**

Spell Weaving

Words go into this spiderweb, one letter per space, starting with the first word, SPIN, and traveling inward around the web. Each new word starts in the box with the clue number, but then continues past the next number because each word overlaps the one before it. For example, Word 2 starts in the box numbered 2 and begins with the letters PIN. Use the letters from one answer to help solve the next one.

Answers, page 184.

Built to Order

By stacking these snowballs to make three-part snowmen, you can form 6 six-letter words related to cold weather. Each head contains one letter, each middle has two letters, and each bottom has three letters. Use one snowball of each size, in order from top to bottom, and write your words in the blank snowmen.

Answers, page 184.

105

Mummy's the Word

Ready for an archaeological dig? Hidden in this grid, reading left, right, up, down, and diagonally, are the 18 things listed here that are associated with ancient Egypt. When you've unearthed them all, read the leftover letters from left to right, starting at the top row, to get a cool fact.

Answers, page 184.

K I N E N O T S A T T E S O R
P A P Y R U S G T U U T L U S
Y C H C L E O P A T R A I I X
R O A N U B I S S G O N F M N
A F R S I R N I O N S M U I I
M B A R A C S D S I S M B O H
I N O L I I S E D K M G O L P
D D H I E R O G L Y P H I C S

ANUBIS	ISIS	PAPYRUS	RUINS
CLEOPATRA	KING TUT	PHARAOH	SAND
CURSE	MUMMY	PYRAMID	SCARAB
GODS	NILE	ROSETTA STONE	SPHINX
HIEROGLYPHICS			TOMB

1.
2.
3.
4.
5.
6.
7.
8.

106

Incredible Edibles

The eight pictures here show objects made out of foods whose names rhyme with them. For example, a fancy dog made from pasta would be a "noodle poodle." Can you identify them all?

Answers, page 184.

The Fright Stuff

Each of the scary words here will take a little digging to read, because some of the bones that make up the letters have been taken away. The whole bony alphabet is shown at the bottom to help you see what's missing and figure out the scary words.

Answers, page 184.

Animal Tracks

By carrying letters down from one set of blanks to the next, you can get the names of 10 animals. The colored paths show you which letters move down, but you'll have to fill in the remaining letters yourself. Colors are used for different letters in different parts of the puzzle. So, for example, even though a red line connects the A in HYENA to an A in the next animal, red may stand for other letters elsewhere.

Answers, page 184.

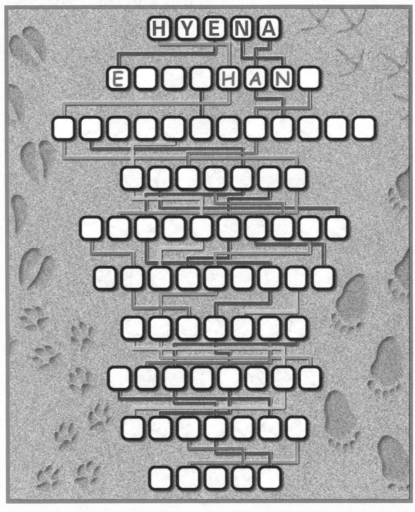

Give Us a Ring

The 18 things listed here will fit into these boxes so that the words all interlock like a crossword puzzle. But everywhere the letters B-E-L-L appear together in the words, they have been replaced in the grid with a picture of a bell. By using the lengths of the words and the places where they cross as a guide, can you put them all in the correct spots? (Ignore spaces and punctuation.) BARBELLS has been placed to help you get started.

Answers, page 185.

BARBELLS	BELLYACHE	COWBELL	POTBELLY
BELL-BOTTOMS	BELLY BUTTON	DOORBELL	REBELLION
BELLBOY	BELLY FLOP	DUMBBELLS	SAVED BY THE BELL
BELLE OF THE BALL	BLUEBELLS	EMBELLISH	SLEIGH BELLS
BELLOWS			YELLOWBELLY

Make the Rounds

Surrounding each picture here are six circles. Start in the circle where the arrow begins and write the name of the picture in the direction the arrow points (just one letter in each circle). Each answer you fill in will provide some letters for the other answers.

Answers, page 185.

```
H T   K H O L D S O C K E B
T I G G S L E N N U F E L X
A S N T M W A A   T N A S O
E I W M A I D M   L C N P B
R E K A H S T L A S E O E R E
W B H O T S L E I E T S A I C
R A M   C E B U T R E N N I
E G R   H H I U U N   K U
T E E T V E K B I L S   L J
A L O O S E L E A F P A P E R
R I E B Y S L E F N R O M R S
G P A B C E S U O H D R I B E
```

BAGEL	**INNER TUBE**	**RING**
BELT	**JUICE BOX**	**SALTSHAKER**
BIRDHOUSE	**KEY**	**SPRINKLER**
BUTTON	**LACE**	**STRAW**
FLUTE	**LOOSE-LEAF PAPER**	**SWISS CHEESE**
FUNNEL	**MASK**	**WATCHBAND**
GRATER	**OLD SOCK**	**WREATH**
	OUTLET	

The Hole Story

Hole-y cow! Hidden in this grid, reading left, right, up, down, and diagonally, are the 22 things listed here that have holes in them. When you've found them all, read the leftover letters from left to right, starting at the top row, to get a cool fact.

Answers, page 185.

Play List

Can you change the word "rock" into "band" one letter at a time? Use each clue to fill in a word that is only one letter different from the word before it. If you get stuck, try solving from the bottom up.

Answers, page 185.

ROCK

It goes between a foot and a shoe

Running a fever

Saint ___ (Santa Claus)

Pleasant and friendly

Number of symphonies Beethoven wrote

Hook, ___, and sinker

Bowling alley

Touch down on the runway

BAND

Diamond Hunt

Ready to step up to the plate? Hidden in this diamond-shaped grid, reading left, right, up, down, and diagonally, are the 20 things listed here that are related to a day at the ballpark. When you've found them all, read the leftover letters from left to right, starting at the top row, to get the answer to the riddle.

Answers, page 185.

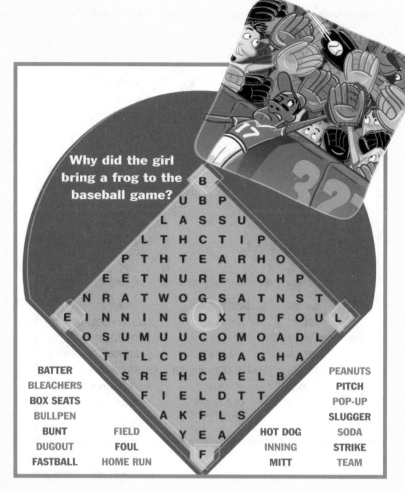

Why did the girl bring a frog to the baseball game?

```
          B
        U B P
      L A S S U
    L T H C T I P
  P T H T E A R H O
E E T N U R E M O H P
N R A T W O G S A T N S T
E I N N I N G D X T D F O U L
O S U M U U C O M O A D L
  T T L C D B B A G H A
    S R E H C A E L B
      F I E L D T T
        A K F L S
          Y E A
            F
```

BATTER
BLEACHERS
BOX SEATS
BULLPEN
BUNT
DUGOUT
FASTBALL

FIELD
FOUL
HOME RUN

HOT DOG
INNING
MITT

PEANUTS
PITCH
POP-UP
SLUGGER
SODA
STRIKE
TEAM

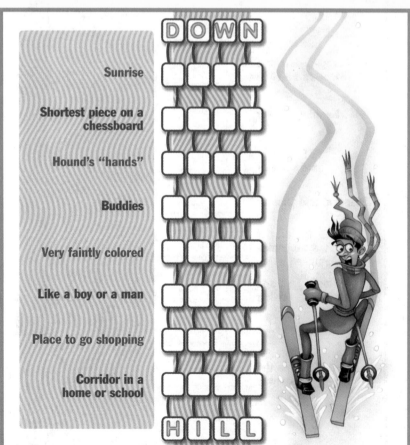

D O W N

- Sunrise
- Shortest piece on a chessboard
- Hound's "hands"
- Buddies
- Very faintly colored
- Like a boy or a man
- Place to go shopping
- Corridor in a home or school

H I L L

Ski Run

Can you glide from "down" to "hill" by changing one letter at a time? Use each clue to fill in a word that is only one letter different from the word before it. If you get stuck, try solving from the bottom up.

Answers, page 185.

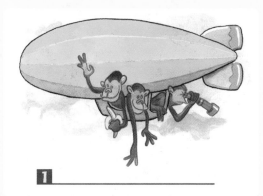

1 _____

2 _____

3 _____

4 _____

5 _____

6 _____

7 _____

8 _____

How's It Going?

The eight pictures here show vehicles and occupants whose names rhyme with each other. For example, an 18-wheeler being driven by a web-footed bird would be a "duck truck." Can you identify them all?

Answers, page 185.

This & That

Each picture in this cross-word shows the first half of a familiar pair, like the lock in "lock and key." Identify each item shown and write the name of its partner in the boxes immediately following the picture. Keep going until you've completed all the pairs.

Answers, page 185.

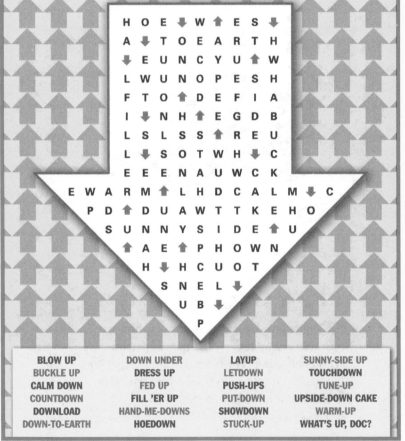

Get the Point?

Listen up! You'll have to look high and low in this arrow, which is filled with 24 things containing "up" or "down." Wherever those words appear in the grid, they've been replaced with arrows (⬇ or ⬆). For example, the answer "blow up" appears in the grid as BLOW ⬆. The words are hidden reading left, right, up, down, and diagonally. When you've found them all, read the leftover letters from left to right, starting at the top row, to find a curious fact.

Answers, page 185.

BLOW UP	DOWN UNDER	LAYUP	SUNNY-SIDE UP
BUCKLE UP	DRESS UP	LETDOWN	TOUCHDOWN
CALM DOWN	FED UP	PUSH-UPS	TUNE-UP
COUNTDOWN	FILL 'ER UP	PUT-DOWN	UPSIDE-DOWN CAKE
DOWNLOAD	HAND-ME-DOWNS	SHOWDOWN	WARM-UP
DOWN-TO-EARTH	HOEDOWN	STUCK-UP	WHAT'S UP, DOC?

The Wordman of Alcatraz

Fitting In

Fill in each row of boxes with the name of one of the objects shown here. One letter from each word has been placed to get you started. When you've filled every box, three pictures will remain unused. Read down the two columns of shaded boxes to discover a phrase that applies to those three pictures.

Answers, page 185.

113

STARS

STRIPES

Flag Daze

Oh say, can you solve this puzzle? These two empty crosswords can be filled in with the 14 words listed here. The top one will contain only things that have stars, and the bottom one will have only things with stripes. Work back and forth between the two crosswords to fit all the words in their proper spots. (Ignore spaces and punctuation.)

Answers, page 185.

BARBER POLE
BAR CODE
BIG DIPPER
CANDY CANE
CHRISTMAS TREE
FILM REVIEW
MOVIE
REFEREE
RUGBY SHIRT
SHERIFF
STATE MAP
TIGER
WIZARD'S CAP
ZEBRA

Jungle Jam

Lurking in this thicket of letters, reading left, right, up, down, and diagonally, are the 18 things listed here associated with rain forests. When you've discovered them all, read the leftover letters from left to right, starting at the top row, to get a cool fact.

Answers, page 186.

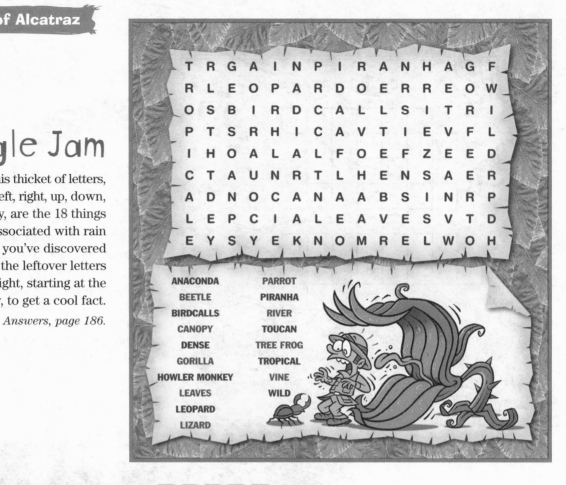

```
T R G A I N P I R A N H A G F
R L E O P A R D O E R R E O W
O S B I R D C A L L S I T R I
P T S R H I C A V T I E V F L
I H O A L A L F O E F Z E E D
C T A U N R T L H E N S A E R
A D N O C A N A A B S I N R P
L E P C I A L E A V E S V T D
E Y S Y E K N O M R E L W O H
```

ANACONDA
BEETLE
BIRDCALLS
CANOPY
DENSE
GORILLA
HOWLER MONKEY
LEAVES
LEOPARD
LIZARD

PARROT
PIRANHA
RIVER
TOUCAN
TREE FROG
TROPICAL
VINE
WILD

114

Play by Play

By carrying letters down from one set of blanks to the next, you can get the names of 10 musical instruments. The colored paths show you which letters move down, but you'll have to fill in the remaining letters yourself. Colors are used for different letters in different parts of the puzzle. So, for example, even though a red line connects the T in the first instrument to a T in the next instrument, red may stand for other letters elsewhere.

Answers, page 186.

1. `_ _ _ _   _ _ _ _`

2. `_ _ _ _ _   _ _ _ _ _`

115

"The fancy-pants word for some punk who's learning the alphabet is 'abecedarian'."

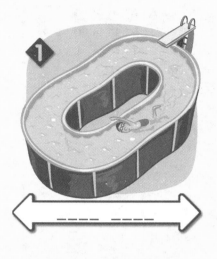

3. `_ _ _   _ _ _`

4. `_ _ _ _   _ _ _ _`

5. `_ _ _ _   _ _ _ _`

6. `_ _ _   _ _ _`

7. `_ _ _ _ _ _   _ _ _ _ _ _`

Going Back on Your Word

Don't forget to look both ways when you describe the pictures here. Each picture can be named with a two-word phrase in which the letters in the two words are in reverse order of each other. For example, a picture showing the highest cooking container in a stack would be "top pot." The blanks below each picture indicate the number of letters in the words. How many of them can you figure out?

Answers, page 186.

8. `_ _ _ _ _ _ _   _ _ _ _ _ _ _`

The Name of the Game

Listed here are 10 sports terms, each from a different sport. Fill in each blank with the name of the term's sport, then look in the grid to find both the terms *and* the sports names, reading left, right, up, down, and diagonally. When you've found them all, read the leftover letters from left to right, starting at the top row, to get a cool fact.

Answers, page 186.

```
            D E E S
        P K B I F T E I
    L B K C O L D A E H L S
    T L S J I W N I W S C L E K
    N I A A A K L M Y R E A A A V G
    F T R B D O R I O T E P T B B A O L
    Z S L E I U E N B A S K E T B A L L
    S P S C N N G T H T M C O U A F
    D A E C R K O O L F X O P P
        B R I O T G S I I K F H
            E C S I N N E T
                I N G G
```

BLITZ _____	LOVE _____
CORNER KICK _____	PUTT _____
DUNK _____	SAFE _____
HEADLOCK _____	SLAP SHOT _____
JAB _____	SPARE _____

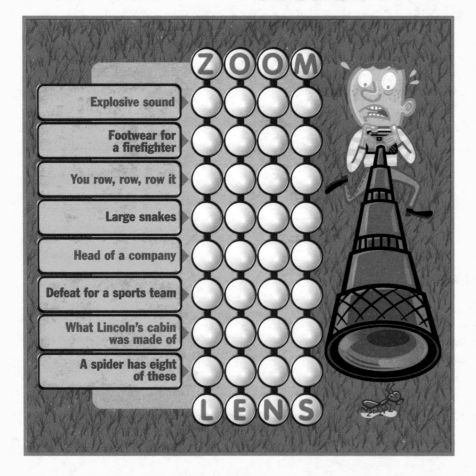

Explosive sound

Footwear for a firefighter

You row, row, row it

Large snakes

Head of a company

Defeat for a sports team

What Lincoln's cabin was made of

A spider has eight of these

ZOOM

LENS

Long Shot

Can you change the word "zoom" into "lens" one letter at a time? Use each clue to fill in a word that is only one letter different from the word before it. If you get stuck, try solving from the bottom up.

Answers, page 186.

Runaround

To fill in this grid, identify each picture and write its name in the bracketed boxes next to it. The words overlap, so every word you fill in will help you get the words next to it. Keep working clockwise to fill in all the boxes.

Answers, page 186.

1. We took a tank of oxygen with us on our climb up the snow-capped mountains.
2. You'd have to be a very foolhardy person to try surviving in the woods all winter.
3. The only thing our snow tires did was grab bits of ice and spit them out behind the car.
4. I got terribly cold on our long hike through the snow.
5. Those big dumb earflaps turned out to be the warmest part of my winter clothing.
6. We'll be able to get around snowy roads easily in the rugged new car I bought.
7. I feel kind of bad that I lost Dad's thermos while we were cross-country skiing.
8. When you go out in the snow without a hat, you lose a lot of heat through your head.

Going Wild

Each of these sentences has the name of a winter animal "hibernating" somewhere inside. All the names are hidden across two or more words. For example, in the first sentence, "fox" appears in "of oxygen." How many animals can you find?

Answers, page 186.

Rated PG

Lights . . . camera . . . abbreviation! This movie lot must be family-friendly, because there are 13 things here that can be described by using the initials PG. For example, that man at the upper left is hitting a "pizza gong." Can you find the 12 other PG-rated things?

Answers, page 186.

118

```
R S O J G N I R R A E M M B E
E P P O I R A O T E S W O A E
E R L L M E W P A R R O T O P
N D O L A E Y E P A T C H S I
A S M Y T N E S N Y D O T I H
C B W R E L K C U B H S A W S
C O S O Y G O U I O A O S N E
U O V G R D O A Y M U T I N Y
B T S E M D H C A N N O N S E
N S T R E A S U R E C H E S T
```

BOOTS	**GOLD**	**PARROT**
BOOTY	**HOIST**	**PLANK**
BUCCANEER	**HOOK**	**ROPES**
CANNON	**JOLLY ROGER**	**SHIP**
COINS	**MAP**	**SWASHBUCKLER**
COVE	**MASTS**	**SWORD**
EARRING	**MATEY**	**TREASURE CHEST**
EYEPATCH	**MUTINY**	**YO HO HO**

Treasure Hunt

Shiver me timbers! Hidden in this grid, reading left, right, up, down, and diagonally, are 24 pirate-related words. When ye be done finding them all, read the leftover letters from port to starboard (that's left to right for ye landlubbers), starting at the top row, to get a cool fact.

Answers, page 186.

119

Batting Order

The 18 things listed here will fit into these boxes so that the words all interlock like a crossword puzzle. But everywhere the letters B-A-T appear together in the words, they have been replaced in the grid with a picture of a bat. By using the lengths of the words and the places where they cross as a guide, can you put them all in the correct spots? (Ignore spaces between words.)

Answers, page 186.

ACROBATICS	**BATMAN**	**BIRDBATH**
ALBATROSS	**BATON**	**COMBAT**
BASEBALL BAT	**BATTALION**	**DEBATE**
BATCH	**BATTER**	**DINGBAT**
BATHING SUIT	**BATTERY**	**SUNBATHER**
BATHROOM	**BATTLESHIP**	**WOMBAT**

Roundabout

Surrounding each picture here are six circles. Start in the circle where the arrow begins and write the name of the picture in the direction the arrow points (just one letter in each circle). Each answer you fill in will provide some letters for the other answers.

Answers, page 186.

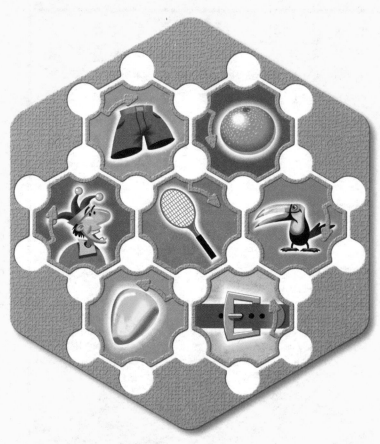

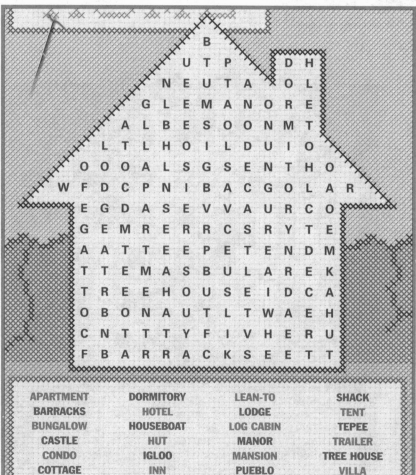

Home Sweet Home

Make yourself at home by looking all over this house, reading left, right, up, down, and diagonally, for the 24 different kinds of homes listed here. When you've found them all, read the leftover letters from left to right, starting at the top row, to get a cool fact.

Answers, page 186.

APARTMENT	DORMITORY	LEAN-TO	SHACK
BARRACKS	HOTEL	LODGE	TENT
BUNGALOW	HOUSEBOAT	LOG CABIN	TEPEE
CASTLE	HUT	MANOR	TRAILER
CONDO	IGLOO	MANSION	TREE HOUSE
COTTAGE	INN	PUEBLO	VILLA

"Get a load of this: One of the longest words you can type using just the top row of a keyboard's letters is 'typewriter'!"

Mad About Hue

This may be a fall festival, but not all the colors are on the leaves. There are 22 things in this scene whose names begin with a color. For example, the bird in the tree is a BLUE JAY. If you can find them all, you pass with flying colors.

Answers, page 187.

121

Sports Casting

By carrying letters down from one set of blanks to the next, you can get the names of 11 sports. The colored paths show you which letters move down, but you'll have to fill in the remaining letters yourself. Colors are used for different letters in different parts of the puzzle. So, for example, even though a red line connects the N in SWIMMING to an N in the next sport, red may stand for other letters elsewhere.

Answers, page 187.

S W I M M I N G
G   M   N   S   I C
W
  B
R
C
S
A

What did the doctor say to the polar bear?

S	Y	C	O	L	L	A	B	N	O	T	T	O	C	S
D	U	H	R	L	O	O	D	R	K	A	S	L	N	O
U	C	A	U	L	I	F	L	O	W	E	R	O	L	O
S	E	L	O	M	A	E	R	C	V	W	W	H	H	L
P	U	K	L	E	G	G	S	I	C	E	B	E	R	G
A	I	G	F	N	S	W	A	N	C	T	E	O	L	I
O	L	L	A	B	E	U	C	U	T	E	O	U	N	M
S	S	S	E	R	D	G	N	I	D	D	E	W	E	E

ANGEL	GLUE
BONE	ICEBERG
CAULIFLOWER	IGLOO
CHALK	PEARL
COTTON BALL	RICE
CREAM	SNOW
CUE BALL	SOAP SUDS
DOVE	SUGAR
EGGS	SWAN
FLOUR	UNICORN
GHOST	WEDDING DRESS

The White Album

You'll need to search far and *white* to find the 22 white things listed here. The words are hidden reading left, right, up, down, and diagonally. When you've found them all, read the leftover letters from left to right, starting at the top row, to get the answer to the riddle.

Answers, page 187.

Else Wear

The good costumes are always harder to find when it gets close to Halloween. That's why this shop offers a second choice that rhymes with each of its most popular costumes. Each kid seen here went in to get one of the neat costumes in the window, but wound up wearing a much less desirable substitute costume whose name rhymes with the one advertised. Can you name the costume each kid wanted and figure out what he or she got instead?

Answers, page 187.

123

Man Hunt

Oh, man! Every place the letters M-A-N appear in the 24 words listed here, they've been replaced with a picture of a man. For example, the word "almanac" can be found in the grid as AL![man]AC. The words are hidden reading left, right, up, down, and diagonally. When you've found them all, read the leftover letters from left to right, starting at the top row, to get a bonus message.

Answers, page 187.

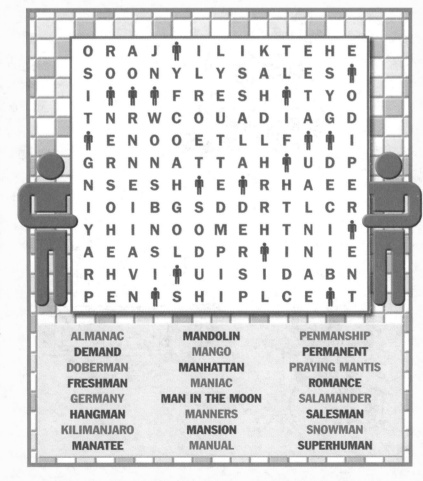

ALMANAC	MANDOLIN	PENMANSHIP
DEMAND	MANGO	PERMANENT
DOBERMAN	MANHATTAN	PRAYING MANTIS
FRESHMAN	MANIAC	ROMANCE
GERMANY	MAN IN THE MOON	SALAMANDER
HANGMAN	MANNERS	SALESMAN
KILIMANJARO	MANSION	SNOWMAN
MANATEE	MANUAL	SUPERHUMAN

The Nutty Professions

Each person here makes a strange living by performing two jobs that rhyme with each other. For example, the man in the first picture is both a PREACHER and a TEACHER. Can you figure out the others?

Answers, page 187.

1

2

3

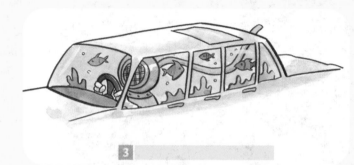

4

5

6

7

8

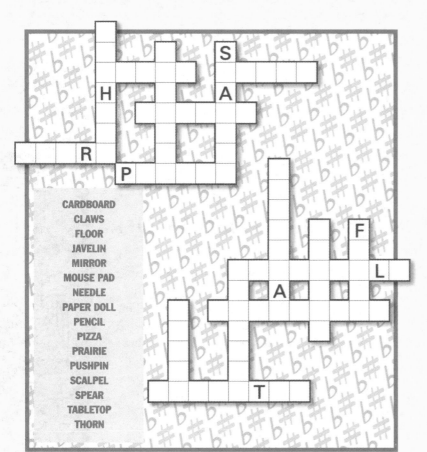

CARDBOARD
CLAWS
FLOOR
JAVELIN
MIRROR
MOUSE PAD
NEEDLE
PAPER DOLL
PENCIL
PIZZA
PRAIRIE
PUSHPIN
SCALPEL
SPEAR
TABLETOP
THORN

Music Boxes

Sharp or flat? In music, that's a half step up (sharp) or down (flat) from a regular note. But in this puzzle, it's a way of deciding where the 16 words here fit into the two empty crosswords. Sharp things from the list go in the top puzzle (which already has the letters of SHARP filled in to help you figure out what fits where). Flat things go in the bottom puzzle (which already has the letters of FLAT filled in). Work back and forth between the puzzles, and you'll be done in no time flat! (Ignore spaces between words.)

Answers, page 187.

Word-Wide Web

This may not look like a typical word search, but it works in the usual way. The 26 words and phrases listed here can be found within this grid of pictures, reading left, right, up, down, and diagonally. For example, the word HANDBAG would be found as a picture of a hand next to a picture of a bag. Can you find everything on the list?

Answers, page 187.

BALLPOINT PEN	CRACKERJACK BOX	FOUNTAIN PEN
BASEBALL DIAMOND	DIAMONDBACK RATTLESNAKE	HAMMERHEAD SHARK
BASKETBALL NET	FAN CLUB	HOUSEFLY
BLOCKHEAD	FAN MAIL	JACKHAMMER
BOOK CLUB	FIRECRACKER	MAILBOX
BOX SPRING	FIRE DRILL	NUTCRACKER
BREADBASKET	FLYPAPER	PAPERBACK BOOK
BUTTERFLY NET	FOOTBALL QUARTERBACK	PEANUT BUTTER
CLUB SANDWICH		TELEPHONE BOOK

Station Identification

Coming up next . . . lots of weird things that can be described by using the initials T.V. For example, that ball on the floor is a "tan volleyball." Can you find 12 other things in this T.V. lineup?

Answers, page 187.

R A I N

Result of stubbing your toe

Most common piece on a chessboard

Cat and dog feet

Encouraging taps on the back

C A T S

Uses scissors

Small simple houses often made of grass

They may be given with kisses

Big oinkers

D O G S

Downpour

Can you get from "rain" to "cats" to "dogs" by changing one letter at a time? Use each clue to fill in a word that is only one letter different from the word before it. If you get stuck, try solving from the bottom up or from the word in the middle.

Answers, page 187.

2 L's	
BUY	_____
CEO	_____
GAZEE	_____
HONOUU	_____
HOY	_____
IAC	_____
INCON	_____
JOY	_____
MA	_____
MOECUE	_____
ONEY	_____
PU	_____

3 L's	
BEY FOP	_____
GOF BA	_____
ITTE EAGUE	_____
JINGE BES	_____
OIPOP	_____
UABY	_____

4 L's	
HIBIY	_____
VOEYBA	_____

```
V P O P I L L O L Y M O O Y
O U U N Y E E D I O A L L P
L L G O L F B A L L N L N O
L I T T L E L E A G U E L L
E M T O I S C I C B Y C L F
Y N A G B U F L U L L A B Y
B L S L L E B E L G N I J L
A A L E L N L O C N I L L L
L A L O I A J G A Z E L L E
L L A L H O N O L U L U A B
```

No L, No L

For this "Noel" Christmas puzzle, all the L's have been removed from the words in the list here. Restore the L's to their proper spots to figure out each entry, and then find it in the grid, reading left, right, up, down, or diagonally. For example, you would add three L's to BEVERY HIS to get BEVERLY HILLS. The words are grouped by the number of L's missing, and two-word entries are separated by a space. When you've found all the words, read the leftover letters from left to right, starting at the top row, to get a bonus message.

Answers, page 187.

5

Sherlogic Holmes

Logic
and sequence
puzzles and
other mysteries
to untangle

Under Wraps

Someone's taken a sneak peek at these holiday gifts. Can you identify each present from just the small portions shown of each word or phrase?

Answers, page 188.

Trick Question

April Fuller wants to buy a trick to play on her friends, but she can't decide which one is best for her. The checklist tells you how she feels about different kinds of tricks. Use all five statements to figure out which gag is the one she should buy.

Answers, page 188.

She wants to eventually play the trick on each of her five best friends.
She won't buy a wet trick if it sprays anyone.
She won't pay over $2.50 for a trick that gets used up.
She likes tricks that do something instead of just sitting there.
She wants a trick that she can use both indoors and outdoors.

Making a Scene

The panels in this comic strip are shown out of order. Can you put them back in the right order so the strip tells a funny story?

Answers, page 188.

131

Arnie's dog has long hair.
Beth's dog is sitting down.
Charlie's dog has a bone-shaped tag.
The only colors on Dora's dog are black and white.
Evan's dog has neither long hair nor spots.
The ears of Francine's dog are standing straight up.

Arnie   Charlie   Dora   Francine

Beth   Evan

Barking Lot

Whose hound is whose? To find out, read the clues and use logic to match each owner with his or her dog. Some of the clues are true for more than one dog, but there's only one way to solve the puzzle.

Answers, page 188.

Making Faces

Mom has used a photo-altering computer program to make a crazy series of changes to a normal portrait of her family. Examine each picture to determine the change she made at each step, then put the pictures in their proper order.

Answers, page 188.

Wild Cards

All of the clubs, from the ace to the king, were dropped in this messy pile of playing cards. Examine what you can see of each card to figure out what it is and which one must be facedown in the center.

Answers, page 188.

 Join the Crowd

The three items in each of these groups have something in common, and it's up to you to figure out what that is. It might be something about the way they look, how they're used, or even how their names sound. When you think you know a group's common theme, look at the pictures at the bottom and find which one item goes with that group.

Answers, page 188.

The loop is the same color as the toe.
It has at least one red stripe.
It has fur trim or a bell, but not both.
She always mends holes in her stocking before she puts it away.

Stocking Stumpers

Although Holly Boughs hangs up her family's stockings each year, she can never remember which one is hers. But she does remember certain important facts about its appearance. Use all four statements to figure out which stocking is hers.

Answers, page 188.

Shutterbug

The panels in this comic strip are shown out of order. Can you put them back in the right order so the strip tells a funny story?

Answers, page 188.

Your Move

Each kid here is playing a different sport, but none of their equipment appears in the pictures. By looking at how the kids are positioned, can you tell which sport each one is playing? Use the list of all the sports, or, for an extra challenge, see how many you can figure out without looking at the list.

Answers, page 188.

134

Taken for a Ride

This family wants to split up and try out six different attractions so they can compare notes afterward. Read the clues and use logic to find out which attraction each person should try first. Some of the clues are true for more than one ride, but there's only one way to solve the puzzle.

Answers, page 188.

Mom wants to get soaked.

Dad wants to go on something for two tickets.

Grandpa wants to go on one of the two highest rides in the park.

Brother wants a ride that goes around in circles.

Sister wants to start in the purple section of the park.

Grandma wants to go on a ride in the same section as a gift shop.

135

Archery	Fencing	Pool
Baseball	Figure skating	Tennis
Basketball	Football	Volleyball
Bowling	Golf	Weight lifting

"Computers can perform diabolically complex tasks, yet I daresay they still cannot be made to understand a simple conversation!"

Floor It!

The painter here painted the floor of this room before removing the objects listed below. As a result, he left unpainted spots where the items used to be. See if you can figure out where everything was, keeping in mind the shapes, number of legs and wheels, and other features of the objects.

Answers, page 188.

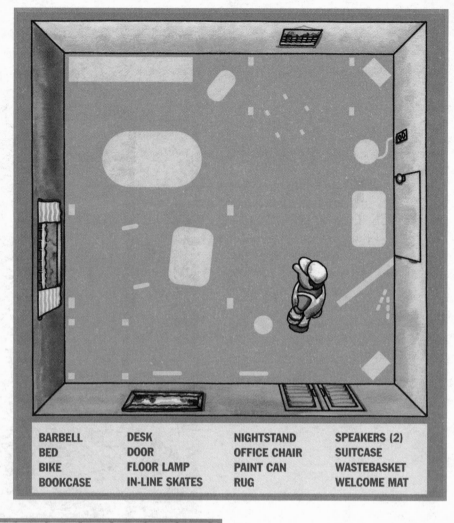

BARBELL	DESK	NIGHTSTAND	SPEAKERS (2)
BED	DOOR	OFFICE CHAIR	SUITCASE
BIKE	FLOOR LAMP	PAINT CAN	WASTEBASKET
BOOKCASE	IN-LINE SKATES	RUG	WELCOME MAT

Pet Peeve

Doggone it! The panels in this comic strip are shown out of order. Can you put them back in the right order so the strip tells a funny story?

Answers, page 188.

He'll only pay over $30 for a sled if it comes with a padded seat.

He'll only get a blue sled if it has racing stripes.

If it doesn't have side handles, it has to have a towrope for pulling.

He doesn't like those round disc sleds.

If it has a high back (for sitting up), he also wants a raised front for tucking his feet under.

Cool Customer

Skip Overhill can't decide which one of these sleds to buy. The checklist tells you how he feels about different kinds of sleds. Use all five statements to figure out which sled is the one for him.

Answers, page 188.

137

Reverse Gear

No, you haven't gone cross-eyed. Some of the things here are normal, but others are shown backward, in mirror image. Using just your memory, can you identify which things are flipped?

Answers, page 188.

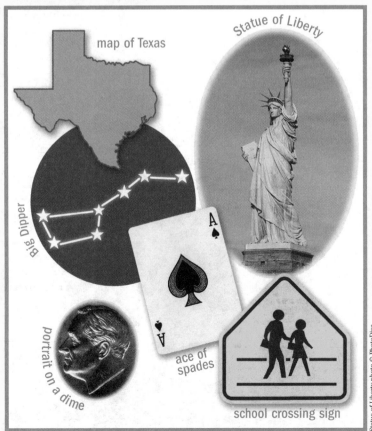

map of Texas

Statue of Liberty

Big Dipper

portrait on a dime

ace of spades

school crossing sign

Wild Thing

A photographer is tracking down the rare and exotic mildebeest, which is one of the six animals in the clearing. But which one is it? Read the only things known about this unusual creature and use those five descriptions to eliminate all but the mildebeest.

Answers, page 188.

138

Its nose and its tail are about the same length.

It has stripes or a long nose, but not both.

If it has a long nose, then it has no white fur.

Its ears are bigger than its eyes.

Of all the animals with eyes the color of the mildebeest's, it has the longest legs.

Hiding Places

This family may need to check every brochure here before they can agree on a vacation spot. Can you identify each place—which may be the name of a city, state, or country—from just the small portions shown of each brochure?

Answers, page 188.

Alex has no hair showing.
Jesse is wearing a hat.
Taylor is dressed in black clothes.
Chris is not holding anything.
Gerry's face is wet.
Pat has only one eye showing.

Scare Wear

It looks like the guests at this costume party are wearing everything but name tags. There's only one way to figure out who's who: Look at the clues and use logic to match the names with the costumes. (The names won't tell you which are boys and which are girls.)

Answers, page 188.

139

Fool Blast

The panels in this comic strip are shown out of order. Can you put them back in the right order so the strip tells a funny story?

Answers, page 188.

That's the Ticket!

When Mattie Nay got to the multiplex, she found these six hit movie posters. To choose which movie to see, she went through her checklist. Use all five statements to figure out which movie is the only one that will work for her.

Answers, page 188.

She likes monster movies, but not if they're rated K.

She likes science fiction, but not if it's a sequel.

She's only allowed to see a movie rated T-15 if it's not a romance.

She likes robots, but not scary ones.

Like most kids, she hates musicals.

Letter Perfect

Each shape here is a close-up of one of the letters in the alphabet shown at the bottom. Examine each close-up and figure out which letter it must be. (All the shapes are shown right side up.) Cross out each alphabet letter as you go, and when you're done, three letters will not have been used. Can you rearrange those letters to spell a common word?

Answers, page 189.

A B C D E F G H I
J K L M N O P Q R
S T U V W X Y Z

In the Present

In all the holiday confusion, the boxes from this comic strip got labeled with the wrong numbers. Can you put the strip back in the right order so it tells a funny story?

Answers, page 189.

141

Fifty-Fifty Split

Can you separate this arrangement of coins into two identical shapes, where each shape contains eight coins that total 50 cents?

Answers, page 189.

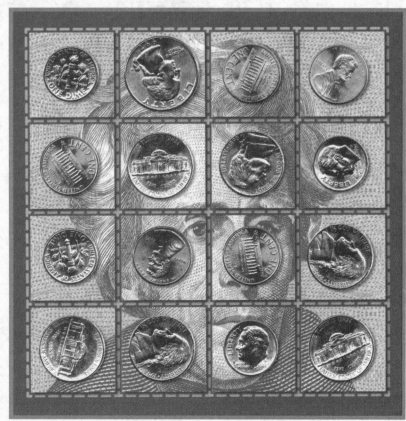

Ifs, Ands & 'Bots

Here in the future, there's a Robot Shack on almost every corner. The question is, which robot is right for you? Today you need a hair-parting robot or a foot-washing robot, but you don't care which. Check your list of preferences to eliminate all but the one perfect robot.

Answers, page 189.

If it's going to wash my feet, I don't want it to be tall.

If it's going to part my hair, it has to have wheels.

I like red robots, and I like robots with clocks. But I don't like robots that are red *and* have clocks.

I don't like propellers, but lights are OK.

If it doesn't make toast, I'm not interested.

Out of Order

The panels in this comic strip are all mixed up. Can you put them back in the right sequence so the strip tells a funny story?

Answers, page 189.

"Mathematicians at many fine universities teach game theory, the fiendishly clever study of how players use strategy to win games."

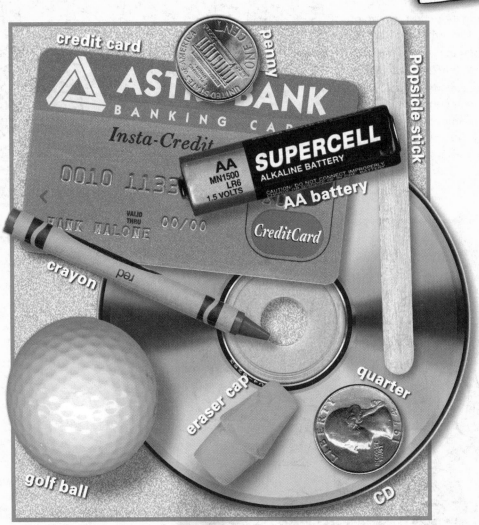

Size 'Em Up

Look carefully at the nine familiar objects here. Three of the items are shown larger than they are in real life, three are smaller, and three are exactly the right size. Without looking at the real things for comparison, can you tell which are which?

Answers, page 189.

Sign Language

The signs on this mall directory are all mixed up. Each store's name has been written in a style that should have been used for another store. For example, the sign for "Ed's VCR Repair" is written in a sports uniform letters style that was meant for "The Sport Spot" sign. Can you figure out how the other names and styles were supposed to be matched?

Answers, page 189.

144

Amelia's snowman is holding something.
Brad's snowman is made of only two sections.
Caitlyn's snowman is wearing a belt.
Drew's snowman has a row of buttons down its front.
Evan's snowman has neither a hat nor a striped scarf.
Faith's snowman has a carrot nose.

Snow Problem

These kids want to remember who built which snowman so they can give back the items they supplied. Read the clues and use logic and observation to find out who built each one. Some clues are true for more than one snowman, but there's only one way to solve the puzzle.

Answers, page 189.

Makeup Test

The 12 pictures here show a trick-or-treater getting into costume—but the pictures are out of order. Figure out the correct order by carefully examining how the makeup and costume are added in each picture. Look sharp—this one's tricky!

Answers, page 189.

Fish Story

Something fishy is going on here—the panels in this comic strip are shown out of order. Can you put them back in the right order so the strip tells a funny story?

Answers, page 189.

6

FrankEinstein

Monster puzzles
to torment
almost any brain
you happen to
have around

Rhyme and Season

In this split scene, 25 summer items on the left rhyme with 25 winter items on the right. For example, the summer girl's HAIR rhymes with the BEAR in the winter scene. If you can find 20, you're a solver for all seasons!

Answers, page 189.

148

Take It or Leave It

This puzzle has two parts. First solve the "word math" equations by identifying each picture and spelling its name in the order shown. To subtract a picture, cross out the letters in its name from the letters you have already written. (For example, CAT + EARS = CATEARS. To subtract SEAT, cross out S, E, A, and T and the remaining letters spell CAR.) Once you've gotten the three final answers, see if you can figure out what they all have in common.

Answers, page 189.

"Human brain about
75 percent water!"

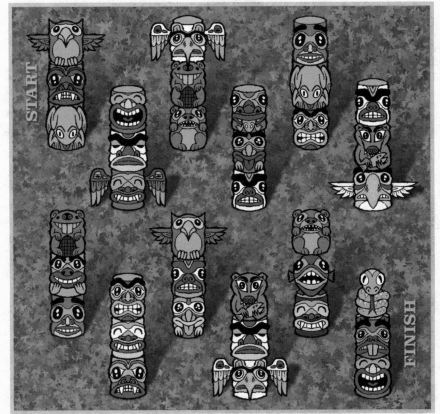

Pole Vault

You'll have to travel from pole to pole to solve this unusual maze. Start by choosing one of the three segments of the first totem pole at top left. Now find the exact same segment somewhere else in the maze and jump to that totem pole. Then choose another segment on that new pole and look for the same segment as that one somewhere else. Keep going until you get to the last totem pole at the bottom right ... but look out for dead ends along the way!

Answers, page 189.

Face to Face

The five kids on top are shown in a different order at the bottom, all in costume for Halloween. They're wearing things like wigs, fake noses, and makeup, but not all their features are covered. Using logic, can you tell who's who?

Answers, page 189.

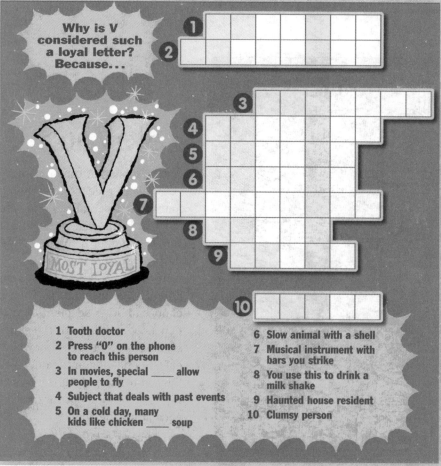

Why is V considered such a loyal letter? Because...

MOST LOYAL

1 Tooth doctor
2 Press "0" on the phone to reach this person
3 In movies, special _____ allow people to fly
4 Subject that deals with past events
5 On a cold day, many kids like chicken _____ soup
6 Slow animal with a shell
7 Musical instrument with bars you strike
8 You use this to drink a milk shake
9 Haunted house resident
10 Clumsy person

Afterwords

The answer to each clue is a word that starts with two consecutive letters of the alphabet, like AB or ST. First read the clues and write your answers in the spaces provided. When you're done, read down the highlighted column to complete the riddle's answer.

Answers, page 189.

Three-for-Alls

Each of these scenes contains three things whose names have all the same letters, but each in a different order (like SPARE, PEARS, and SPEAR). Can you find all the scrambled threesomes?

Answers, page 189.

Take Your Pick

Five familiar items have had their names broken into three pieces. To find out what they are, identify all the pictures. Then choose one word from each column, in order (starting with the left column), and combine them to get the name of a familiar object. For example, if there were a CARD in the first column, a BOARD in the second, and a BOX in the third, they could be combined to form CARDBOARD BOX. Can you figure out all five items?

Answers, page 190.

Gift Boxes

In this category-based word search, find the 20 words in the grid of letters that complete the table at the bottom, one word per box. Each word starts with one of the letters in the word GIFTS and fits into one of the four categories given at the bottom. The words can be found in the grid reading left, right, up, down, and diagonally. When you've found them all, read the leftover letters from left to right, starting at the top row, to get a bonus message.

Answers, page 190.

```
E N O G L W T G I R A F F E
H P U A T L Y O A I U O V G
E M A G O S U T T N O H I E
S O U T H D A K O T A E S O
P K F U Z Z L X S E E U A R
L N L R W F R A E S P G G G
T U F L O R I D A T P N E I
I K D L H G U P B I E O S A
G S D R A C X E D N I T U R
E E E T D O G L U E T A K E
R A B O I W S R O S S I C S
```

ANIMALS	U.S. STATES	PARTS OF THE BODY	SCHOOL SUPPLIES
G	G	G	G
I	I	I	I
F	F	F	F
T	T	T	T
S	S	S	S

All Set

This grid can be divided into four sections so that the four items in each section have something in common. Each square must share at least one edge with another square in its section. The common element could have to do with their names, their parts, or other connections. For example, a paint roller, umbrella, tennis racket, and suitcase all have handles. Can you identify all four groups?

Answers, page 190.

It
All Adds Up

First, identify the two words illustrated in each "equation." Then add up their letters by scrambling them together to spell the name of one of the items pictured at the bottom. For example, pictures of TAPE + SUN would equal a picture of PEANUTS (which uses all the letters in a different order). Can you make them all add up?

Answers, page 190.

153

Get
Cracking!

Each of these lists has been translated into its own code. In the first list, for example, a V represents W, so fill in W wherever you see a V. Every letter you get, and patterns like repeated letters, will help you figure out the rest of the code. Hint: Start by thinking of something that might fit into one of the lists, then see if any of the entries have that same letter pattern.

Answers, page 190.

AT THE AMUSEMENT PARK
Example: Souvenir stand

UBCCXU PBOGNXU
W
VONXUGCTEX

DXUUTG VKXXC

PBNNBM POMEH

GLXX-ZOCC

FXUUH-YB-UBSME

DTUXVBULG GKBV

ZSFAXU POUG

DSM KBSGX

NTPLXN ZBBNK

BLACK-AND-WHITE THINGS
Example: Penguin

YJPPKG IMBPK

AMKUU ZJKAKU

CPQ ZMCECLGBZM
              B
KJLME DBPP

UYRTY

DBG ACQK

AGCUUICGQ ZRNNPK

NKDGB

BAK CV UZBQKU

ZJBTC YKXU

Snow Way

To solve this unusual maze, you may move from one hexagonal space to any adjacent hexagonal space—but only if it has the same color or contains an identical snowflake to the one you're on. Start on the snowflake in the top space. From there you may move to any of the three surrounding it—the purple ones are the same color, and the green one is the same flake. Keep moving until you reach the flake in the bottom space.

Answers, page 190.

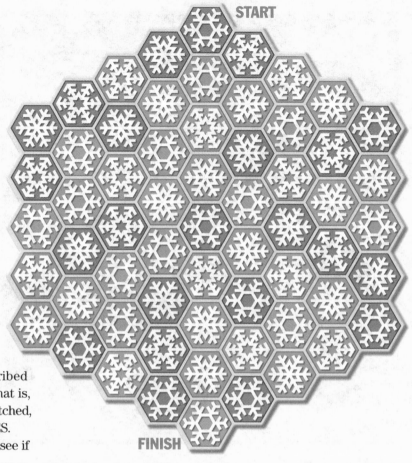

START

FINISH

Switcheroos

Each pair of pictures here can be described with "spoonerisms" of each other—that is, two words that have their first sounds switched, like CANNED GRAPES and GRAND CAPES. Look carefully at each pair of pictures and see if you can guess the spoonerisms.

Answers, page 190.

154

1 _____

2 _____

3 _____

4 _____

5 _____

6 _____

George and his parents sat in a single-engine [1] plane , flying to Athens for a [2] _____ of summer fun.

But an [3] _____ and a half before arriving, they had engine trouble and made an emergency landing on a tropical desert [4] _____ in the middle of the [5] _____ .

At first, George didn't care [6] _____ or not they ever got rescued. He [7] _____ delicious fruit all day and played in the hot [8] _____ . The [6] _____ was always beautiful and warm.

But after [7] _____ months, he felt [2] _____ in the knees. He could hardly [9] _____ his clothes anymore because he didn't [10] _____ as much as he used to. He dreamed of eating a hot fudge [11] _____ . And since there was nothing to do, he was just [1] plain [12] _____ .

George told his parents, "You [13] _____ something? I used to like living here, but now [4] _____ be glad to leave."

One day the pilot came to the family wiping oily black [14] _____ from his hands and announced he had fixed the engine. By that [11] _____ morning, everyone was getting back on [12] _____ , and George's dad said "Don't worry, [8] _____ . We'll soon be back [9] _____ we belong."

"You mean [3] _____ home?" said George. "[13] _____ [10] _____ ! Not until I get to [5] _____ [14] _____ !"

Hear Here

In this story, 14 pairs of homophones (words that have different meanings and spellings, but that sound the same) have been removed and replaced with numbered blanks. When you come to a blank, find its numbered mate to help you figure out both missing words. Pair #1 has been filled in to help you get started.

Answers, page 190.

155

156

Common Sense

The three items in each group here have something in common, but it's up to you to figure out what it is. For example, if we showed a truck, a bugler, and a rhinoceros, the answer would be "horns." How many of the groups can you figure out? The answer may not always be something you can see here.

Answers, page 190.

Hex Mix

To create the objects in her book of spells, this witch will transform each item on the table by adding a letter from one potion and mixing it up with the letters in the name of the item on the table. For example, a "D" potion added to an ORGAN would make a DRAGON. Can you mix everything up properly? All the potions will be used once.

Answers, page 190.

Letterheads

Each picture here stands for a common word that, when spoken out loud, sounds like a letter performing an activity. For example, the first picture shows the word ENCLOSING (N closing). Can you get the others?

Answers, page 190.

Spinning Wheel

Each of the pictures here can be identified with a four-letter name. Once you have each name, write it in the grid above in the direction shown by its arrow, starting at the outside and moving in toward the center in an arc. One answer has been filled in to get you started.

Answers, page 190.

When did the sign painter stop
painting the word "soccer"?
WHEN HE . . .

TONIGHT
SOCC

BB
DD
EE
FF
GG
LL
MM
NN
OO
PP
RR
SS
TT
ZZ

Animal that gathers nuts in its cheeks
The color of a lime
You can blow one of these out of gum
Natural wonder on the Niagara River
Place for pieces like pawns and castles
Punctuation mark, like the one
in this clue
Ketchup container
Where you sleep and keep your stuff

A lot of cars on one road
Place to get a pepperoni pie
Slow, steady running
Words like hot and cold,
or top and bottom
You can change to a new one
with your TV remote
Climbing device for firefighters
or housepainters

Think Twice

The answer to each clue is a word
that contains a pair of double
letters. First read the clues and find
the only spot where each answer will
fit. When you're done, read down the
highlighted column to complete the
riddle's answer.

Answers, page 191.

Rhyme Wave

Everything pictured here is something that rhymes with its neighbor.
For example, the banana PEEL rhymes
with WHEEL. But look again—the wheel
can also be identified as a TIRE, which
rhymes with a word describing the
picture after it. Continue along the
path until you've made all the rhymes. You'll
need to identify each picture with two
different words to complete the puzzle.

Answers, page 191.

Way to Go

By carrying letters down from one set of blanks to the next, you can get the names of 10 kinds of transportation, new and old. The colored paths show you which letters move down, but you'll have to fill in the remaining letters yourself. Colors are used for different letters in different parts of the puzzle. So, for example, even though a red line connects the R in TRUCK to an R in the next vehicle, red may stand for other letters elsewhere.

Answers, page 191.

Shore Thing

Building a sandcastle is no day at the beach! The eight pictures here are shown out of order. Examine each picture carefully to place it in its proper sequence, from first to last.

Answers, page 191.

Drop by Drop

By dropping a letter from the name of one item in each picture, you can get the name of another item in the scene. Then you can drop a letter from *that* item to get a third item in the scene. For example, PLANET could become PLANE and PLANE could become PANE, if they were all pictured in one scene. The letter that's dropped in each step can come from the beginning, middle, or end of the words. Can you find all the trios?

Answers, page 191.

161

Rhyme Spree

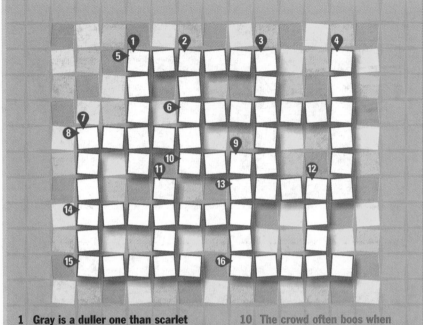

In this crossword, each clue not only describes the answer but also contains a word that rhymes with the answer word. For example, Clue 1, "Gray is a duller one than scarlet," leads to the answer COLOR, since "color" rhymes with "duller" and also answers the clue. It's up to you to figure out which is the rhyming word. The arrows point in the direction each word should be entered.

Answers, page 191.

1. Gray is a duller one than scarlet
2. This four-footed mammal may have one hump or two
3. You might store your equipment in your locker after playing this team sport
4. It's a real hassle to clean this enormous house built for a king
5. Cowboys make it a practice never to sit on this spiny plant
6. You might have to light a few of these before a candle catches fire
7. This writing instrument is used to trace a stencil
8. You hear a dial tone when you pick up this calling device
9. This word describes the taste of a candy treat
10. The crowd often boos when they watch their team do this
11. This sticky goo can fasten things together permanently
12. This part of the male peacock is dazzlingly beautiful
13. It's what you did if you jotted down a note
14. You can gain more knowledge by attending this after high school
15. It's the type of paper you find in most notebooks
16. When designing a book cover, it's vital to include this

"Egyptians thought heart do thinking, so threw out brain when making mummy!"

Round Trip

First identify each object shown here with a four-letter word. Then fill in those words in order around the loop so that each word is only one letter different from the one before it. (If you get stuck, try solving in the other direction.) For example, the first word, BACK, is one letter different from the second word, BUCK. Cross off pictures as you add words, and you'll end up right where you started.

Answers, page 191.

 Wild Flowers

Each of these six blooms is made from the letters in the name of a flower. The letters are scrambled, and some of them are even upside down. In addition, each set of letters appears six times. For example, Flower 1 contains the letters R, S, I, and I, and the answer is IRIS. See if you can identify the others.

Answers, page 191.

163

BACK

BUCK

Driving Wild

The answer to the riddle will be spelled out across the three rows of boxes. To get that answer, fill in the boxes to complete a three-letter word in each column. In some cases, you may have more than one choice, so work both across and down to decide which letter to use. (In the first box, a D will make the only possible word, DUO, but you have more than one choice for the second box.) Be careful! You might want to use a pencil with a good eraser.

Answers, page 191.

What did the safari park put on the road to keep people driving straight?

Let It Snow

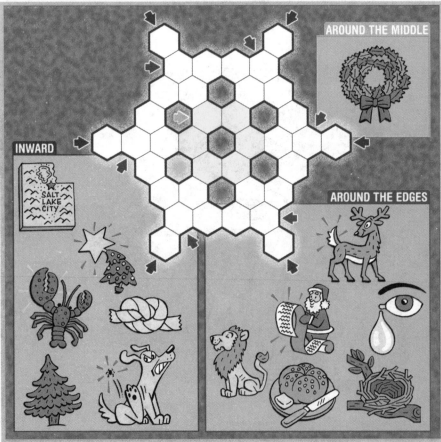

AROUND THE MIDDLE

INWARD

SALT LAKE CITY

AROUND THE EDGES

To fill in this snowflake grid, start by entering the six-letter word indicated by the "around the middle" picture, beginning at the yellow arrow and going clockwise in the yellow spaces. All the other pictures illustrate four-letter words, and it's up to you to figure out where they belong in the grid. The "inward" words follow the directions of the green arrows, beginning at the snowflake's points and ending in the yellow spaces in the middle. The "around the edges" words follow the directions of the red arrows, with one word on each of the snowflake's six edges.

Answers, page 191.

164

Presents and Absence

Some gifts would be perfect if they only had a little extra something. The gifts that these people got are each missing one letter, which turned them into completely different items from what they wanted. For example, a person who wanted a TIRE for his car might have gotten a TIE instead, because his gift was missing an R. To solve the puzzle, first match each gift with the person who got it, and then figure out which letter was dropped in each. When you have all eight missing letters, unscramble them to spell a common word that might describe these inappropriate gifts.

Answers, page 191.

Gifts

166

Grid:

```
W E T W S U O R E G N A D
U D O R H E A V Y A L L T
D N O N U Y I H E T S H F
E U S S O T C K R A D Y E
O O O U A I H T O G N O L
P F N G R P N A O U A S I
T G E X C E L L E N T T E
G N O R W O F L R A S R E
```

On the Contrary

Some words have two meanings, so they can also have two different kinds of opposites. For each word listed, think of two unrelated words that are each its opposite and find them in the grid. For example, given the word GO, you would look for both STOP and COME. The words can be found reading left, right, up, down, and diagonally. When you've found them all, read the leftover letters from left to right, starting at the top row, to get a bonus message.

Answers, page 192.

HARD	_____ _____	POOR	_____ _____
LIE	_____ _____	POSITIVE	_____ _____
LIGHT	_____ _____	RIGHT	_____ _____
LOST	_____ _____	SAFE	_____ _____
OLD	_____ _____	SHORT	_____ _____

Jeepers! Peepers!

Ever get the feeling you're being watched? This guy's feeling is right: He *is* being watched by eight pairs of eyes peering at him from various places around the room. The views above show what each set of eyes sees from its hiding spot. Can you figure out which pair of eyes sees each view?

Answers, page 191.

167

Why don't elephants like to use computers?

Gray Matter

This puzzle has two parts. First, name the seven pictures and figure out where to put the words in the crossword. Second, transfer the letters from the crossword to the numbered boxes at the bottom to get the answer to the riddle.

Answers, page 192.

TRADITIONAL
PLANETS

J

W

NUMBERS FROM
ONE TO TEN

COLORS OF
THE RAINBOW   I

Z   THE SEVEN
DWARFS

168

Box Sets

Each of the miniature crosswords here can be filled in with the complete set of words that make up the category shown—and it's up to you to supply those words. One letter in each puzzle has been placed to help you get started. Use the lengths of words and the letters where they cross to fill in every word in each set.

Answers, page 192.

Get the Picture?

The noted painter Art Starr claims that his latest masterpiece makes his boldest statement ever. But one brave critic says, "The way I see it, this painting is a joke!" Take a good look at the painting and see if you can tell what the critic means. Be careful, this one's tricky!

Answers, page 192.

Answers

It's Astro-Logical

1. C   4. A   7. Sleeping
2. G   5. B   8. D
3. F   6. E   9. H

Brrr!

Objects: Bridge, bricks, brook, branch, braid, bracelet, brush, broth, broccoli, bread, bride, broom, braces, brain, brothers, breath, bronco.

Tree's Company

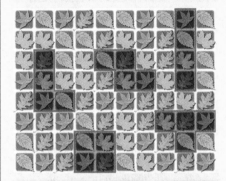

Look! Up in the Sky!

The matching pairs are indicated by letters. The one-of-a-kind dragon kite and the group of three flame kites are shown in color.

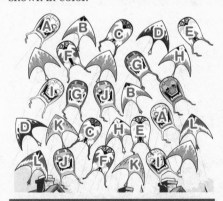

Trick or Trade

The musketeer has the vampire's fangs.
The angel has the football player's helmet.
The hippie has the geisha's fan.
The matador has the hippie's glasses.
The football player has the matador's cape.
The vampire has the astronaut's gloves.
The geisha has the musketeer's hat.
The astronaut has the angel's wings.

Out to Lunch

Mistakes: Nighttime in one window and daytime in another; menu cover upside down; waitress writing with spoon; waitress wearing one shoe; cashier playing game on cash register; sign says "HAVE A A NICE DAY"; pie case is round at top and square at bottom; spaceship in pie case; girl drinking ketchup; man's clothes backward; man eating soup from hat; man with menu in front has three hands; waitress's tray is unbalanced; post missing from stool; man sipping from empty glass; door into kitchen swings out at top even though waitress is pushing on it; nurse's cap on waitress; waitress pouring coffee into cereal; woman eating from dog bowl; cake has both three layers and two layers; salt and pepper labels switched; sock with cook's orders; cook flipping whole egg; cook holding plate upside down.

Instant Replay

Changes to picture on right: Man's tongue shifts sides; fielder's mitt becomes catcher's mitt; camera becomes binoculars; spilled popcorn becomes spilled peanuts; woman's earring changes color; drink becomes ice-cream sundae; man's glasses change shape; man's watch disappears; mascot on hat changes direction; scorecard becomes crossword puzzle; "GO TEAM!" on banner becomes "GO AT 'EM!"; stripe appears on kid's shirt; bald man gets hair; squirted mustard becomes ketchup.

Double Take

Snow Business

The perfect snowflakes are 2 and 7. The mistakes in the others are circled.

Simply Smashing

The matches are 2 and 8.
Differences:
1. Extra fang
3. No hair on arm
4. Shift in piece at middle right
5. Wart removed
6. Thumb removed
7. Two pieces combined at top left

Even Steven

Two: glue, screw, shoe
Four: core (of apple), door, oar
Six: bricks, chicks, sticks
Eight: crate, gate, plate
Ten: hen, men, pen

Foiled Again!

1. FORK
2. OCTOBER
3. MAID
4. UMBRELLA
5. SOCK
6. LINCOLN
7. VIOLIN
8. BOWLING
9. DOG
10. BASKET
11. HAMMER
12. SHARK
13. CAST
14. BEARD
15. LADDER
16. RAKE
17. GLASSES
18. DETECTIVE

The "leftover" letters spell this message: The painter was caught red-handed.

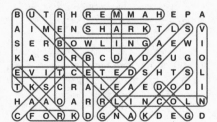

169

Wrap Group

The wrapping paper should be the one with the holly (the roll of paper in the middle) and the ribbon should be dark green.

Insiders

1. Saltshaker
2. Birdhouse
3. Toaster
4. Washing machine
5. Hole at a miniature golf course
6. Orange-drink carton

Junked Mail

Front: Washington has a bow tie; Jefferson is smiling; Lincoln has a mohawk hairdo; the White House is on a cliff; "Rushmore" is misspelled. Back: Rushmore is in South Dakota, not New Mexico; Rushmore is not a natural formation; Fred can't be an aunt; 4 days must include at least 3 nights, not 2; "scene" should be "seen"; "would" is repeated; "here were" should be "were here"; P.S. could not have been written if pen was lost; there is no June 31 (postmark date); stamp should say "Eagle," not "Beagle"; there are no 18½-cent stamps; street address is missing; Honolulu is not in New York; zip code is too short.

It's All Downhill From Here

Mistakes: Moose has two different kinds of antlers; framed picture is hung from its side; picture's snow scene has a palm tree; bowling pins in fireplace; one ski against wall is pointed at both ends; one ski pole has a fork; bearskin rug has leopard spots; icicles are inside lodge; couch's stripes change color between woman's legs; seated man has three hands; "SKIIING" book on table is misspelled with three I's; people on ski lift are riding down instead of up; woman on ski lift is wearing in-line skates; cherry on top of mountain; kid going down ski jump is dressed for swimming; sky changes color in windowpane at far right; man with two broken arms has crutches he doesn't need; woman on stairs is holding mug upside down; a post from stairway's rear banister goes in front of the front banister; cuckoo is too big to fit through clock's door; 3 and 9 on clock are switched; one clock counterweight is a fish.

Flipping Out

The matches are B and E.
Differences:
A. Piece under back wheels is missing
C. Shorts are yellow
D. Helmet stripe is solid
F. Lightning bolt is reversed
G. Sleeves are shorter

Hot Lines

1. Backpack, baseball mitt
2. Sports radio, inflatable ring
3. Sunglasses, pants
4. Tank top, flip-flops
5. Visor, swim fins
6. Scuba mask, watch

Spare Change

Changes to picture on right: Orange triangle is blue; one extra pin in center alley; glasses on man cleaning; broom becomes mop; woman's hair becomes wavy; shirt reads GARBAGE instead of GARAGE; middle ball in ball return changes color; boy's cap has shorter bill; shoes in boy's hand are tied; straw in cup on table loses bend; pizza moves on plate; girl writing with other hand; chair bases are separated; hot dog has mustard; orange ball is rotated; man's sleeves are longer; green and yellow balls are pushed together.

Snowed In

Get Real!

Painting: A—raised eyebrow; B—watch on wrist; C—cloud moved; D—perfect copy; E—hands reversed
Dollar: A—round seal missing; B—perfect copy; C—ONE and BUCK reversed; D—portrait reversed; E—bow tie added
Urn: A—perfect copy; B—trident instead of spear; C—top piece missing; D—colors reversed at bottom; E—triangle on shield instead of star
Stamp: A—light beam in front missing; B—baseball cap on engineer; C—road instead of tracks; D—yellow smokestack; E—perfect copy

Bat Attitude

Ticket or Leave It

Mistakes: Medium-sized popcorn is most expensive; free butter is not free; money has two different values; counterman is reaching arm through glass; soda machine has winding spray; clocks are for sale in candy counter; customer bought pile of socks; boy is drinking from popcorn bucket; customers are exiting through closed door; trash receptacle has grid over hole; "Cinema" is misspelled "Cimena"; movie poster changes "Leopard" to "Leotard"; theater entrance has men's room sign; blond kid is holding drink upside down; "Coming soon" has three O's in "soon"; Babe Ruth is depicted as football player, not baseball player; woman viewing poster has one long sleeve and one short sleeve; boy in white shirt is wearing one in-line skate; rope partition is not attached to pole; ticket taker is missing arm; edges of torn ticket halves do not match; woman's hand has six fingers.

Roundup

Objects: Silo, flamingo, volcano, tornado, tuxedo (on riding man), lasso, limo, superhero, domino, rhino, bronco, banjo, cello, buffalo, sombrero, mosquito, taco, tomato, photo, rodeo.

One, Two, Tree

The matching pairs are indicated by letters. The one-of-a-kind ornament is circled in yellow, and the group of three is circled in white.

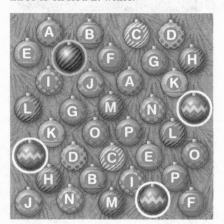

Triangle Trio

The pictures represent tea, eye, and bee—which are all letters of the alphabet when said out loud.

Rhapsody in Boo

Objects: Book, booties, telephone booth, bamboo, booger (baby ghost), booster seat (baby ghost), pocketbook, baboon, Daniel Boone, caboose, boomerang, boom box, boot.

Birds of a Feather

The matching pairs are:
A: Speckled area is lower
B: Three tail feathers
C: Yellow feathers on wing tip
D: No red dot on back of head
E: Longer crest feathers on head
F: Beak has sharper curve
G: Fewer speckles on chest
The remaining bird has no match.

Look Out Below

Differences in reflection: Crashing boys are switched; crashing boy's gloves are mittens; reflected number 6 should look like a backward 9; long tail on hat is shorter; purple pants change style; girl pulling dog has different hairstyle; leash is missing; dog has different spots; reflection of man in couple is not aligned; skate of woman in couple is different color; sleeping dog has no reflection; leaping boy's pants are different color; leaping boy's skate blades are missing; sitting girl has glasses; sitting girl's jacket patch is different; falling man has in-line skates.

Cut It Out!

1. Dictionary
2. Calendar
3. Telephone book
4. Map
5. Restaurant menu
6. Cash register receipt
7. Recipe
8. Comics page
9. Eye chart

Dinner's on Me!

The matches are 1 and 5.
Differences:
2. Seeds on bun are missing
3. Extra french fry
4. Ketchup on burger patty
6. Pickle is on top of burger patty
7. Design around plate edge is wavy
8. Toothpick decoration is yellow

The Dr. Is In

Objects: Drapes, drawbridge, driver, drumstick, Dracula, drawstring, drawer, dryer, dropper, dream (on magazine), dress, drum, drink, drip, drain, dragon, drill.

It's No Use!

The missing items are:
1. Sink: drain
2. Belt: metal prong that fits through holes when belt is worn
3. Pot: lid handle
4. Spray bottle: tube to draw liquid into sprayer
5. Gumball machine: opening where gumball comes out
6. Pencil: lead
7. Shirt: buttonholes
8. Wheelbarrow: support legs

Mirror, Mirror

Differences in reflection: Airplane reflected wrong; lost balloon becomes boy's head; theater clock hands reflected wrong; fireman has hot dog; ladder rungs missing; hose hooked to elephant's trunk; elephant's legs reflected wrong; "Circus is coming" becomes "going"; bird has pizza; flag reflected wrong; streetlight becomes showerhead; window shade is upside down; cactus is upside down; R and S in *Toy Story* reflected wrong; blue and orange triangles on theater switch colors; hair of woman at theater changes color; EAT sign reflected wrong; pants of man holding framed mirror change color; person's reflection in framed mirror and placement of banana change; backseat passenger's head reflected wrong; dash in license plate moves position; tire has two tacks; hydrant water sprays from sidewalk; scooter kid's hairstyle changes; kid's shirt stripes reflected wrong; alligator has toothbrush; dog loses rear leg.

Band Over Backward

Mistakes: Paint can labeled "red" has green paint; lightbulb is upside down; cymbal is a hat; one drumstick is a chicken drumstick; guitar neck is a ruler; guitar has no strings; guitarist has six fingers on his left hand; part of the microphone stand is missing; pattern on the guitarist's shirt changes; neck of bass guitar is both behind and in front of ladder; amp is a fish tank; bass wire turns into garden hose.

Hide-and-Squeak

Drawn to Scale

DO (picture 6): dog, doll, donut
RE (picture 3): refrigerator, reindeer, remote
MI (picture 1): microphone, milk, mime
FA (picture 5): fan, fangs, faucet
SO (picture 2): soap, socks, sombrero
LA (picture 4): ladder, lake, laundry
TI (picture 7): tickets, tie, tiger

Space Case

The matching pairs are indicated by letters. The one-of-a-kind ship is shown in color.

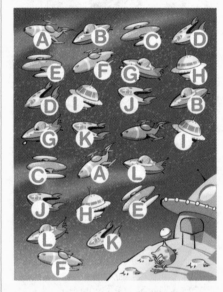

Eye Bogglers

1. Soda can
2. Lamp
3. Broom
4. Hammer
5. Videotape
6. Dictionary
7. Bike helmet
8. Umbrella
9. Can opener

Call of the Wild

The animals are all hidden in the form of words, as shown here.

Look Twice

Haunted Hike

The house the trick-or-treaters live in is marked with a star.

Animal Crackers

Mistakes: Fish is a piece of wrapped candy; "S" in "Pet Shop" doesn't face the same way as rest of sign; store is selling collars for fish; "Fish Food Sale" sign shows a price increase; bird is in a bag of water; boy is a chimp; red bird and perch are outside of cage; blue bird's cage chain is missing a link; blue bird's cage has basketball and net; large fish tank's water is at an angle; fish is wearing glasses; rhino is in cage; fish and water in cage; cat has a windup key; girl's shirt has a long sleeve and a short sleeve; hamster is reading the paper; dog is upside down; turtle has two heads; turtle has taillights and a license plate; snake's pattern changes between branches; snake's tongue is a fork; "Please do not tap on on glass" sign repeats "on"; boy has three arms; cat is half lizard; computer mouse is in mouse cage.

Garden Party

The four fake gnomes are starred.
Differences:
1. Shirt longer
2. Eyebrows different
3. Mustache added
4. Beard shorter
5. No points on shoes
6. Belt added
7. Hat color changed
8. Sleeves longer

Tic Tac Show

Tic: brick, chick, pick, stick
Tac: sack, stack (of paper), track, yak
Toe: bow, crow, hoe, snow

2: RIDDLE GREEN MEN

A Piece of the Action

The answer to the riddle is: **There are so many fans.**

Crunch Time

The answer to the riddle is: **Because he wanted a light lunch.**

Gross-Outs

1. Spool, pool, stool
2. Bat (baseball bat and flying bat)
3. Scarf, scale
4. Warts, straw
5. Orange, gargoyle, boomerang
6. Birthday cake, jack-o'-lantern

The answer to the riddle is:
COFFIN SYRUP.

ABC Ya Later!

1. A, J, K
2. F, H, P, S, T, Y
3. I, V, X
4. C, Z
5. G, U, X
6. S, T, M
7. R, Y
8. N, D, Q (nickel, dime, quarter)

The final answer is: BELOW.

Check It Twice

The answer to the riddle is: POLE VAULT.

The differences in the bottom picture, from left to right, are: blanket on toy horse is green; glasses are round; candle is shorter; elf's shoe is curly; snowflake in window has moved down; doorknob has changed to a handle; Santa's suit has a pocket; long and short icicles in doorway are switched; pole's stripes have changed direction.

What Not

1. Tarantula—Although a tarantula's bite can be painful, it contains no poison.
2. Can opener—The can opener was invented in 1870, about 50 years after the invention of the can. Roller skates and the piano were both invented around 1710.
3. Ostrich—Ostriches are from Africa.
4. Torpedo—The torpedo is not named after a person. The other items were invented by Count Ferdinand von Zeppelin and Roy Jacuzzi.
5. Using a yo-yo—In 1971, two astronauts from Apollo 14 tested the moon's gravity by hitting golf balls and throwing a javelin, but nobody tried to yo-yo.
6. Tyrannosaurus—The Tyrannosaurus rex is from the Cretaceous period, which immediately followed the Jurassic period. The stegosaurus and pterodactyl lived in both periods.
7. Pretzel—Pretzels have been eaten in Europe for over 1,000 years. Both the ice-cream cone and the hot dog (with bun) have their origins in St. Louis, Missouri, in the late 1800s.
8. Nevada—Nevada has no major league sports team (as of this book's publication). Oregon has basketball's Portland Trail Blazers, and North Carolina has basketball's Charlotte Bobcats, football's Carolina Panthers, and hockey's Carolina Hurricanes.

Just Say the Word

The answer to the riddle is: GROAN MEN.

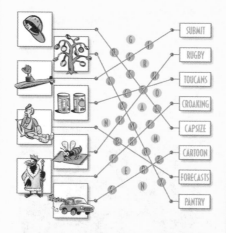

Look Both Ways

The answer to the riddle is: HAIRCUTS.

H	E	A	D
E	A	S	E
A	S	I	A
D	E	A	R

C	L	A	M
L	U	R	E
A	R	T	S
M	E	S	S

Downhill Run

The answer to the riddle is: A COLD SPELL.

1. LEA VES
2. CAR TON
3. BUT LER
4. COO KED
5. DUN CES
6. SPI DER
7. LAD LES

Knockouts

1. Mouse, bat
2. Tent, window
3. Violin, kite, yo-yo
4. Sundae
5. Pocket, rocket
6. Peanut, egg

The answer to the riddle is: FOOTBALL QUARTERBACK (foot, ball, quarter, back).

Scavenger Haunt

The answer to the riddle is: It was over his head.

Find Dining

The answer to the riddle is: **Look for a fork in the road.**

Hear and There

The pairs are: circular saw and bee (buzz), pen and mouse (click), whip and bat striking ball (crack), horn and goose (honk), keys and bells (jingle), bear and stomach (growl), balloon and popcorn (pop), flat tire and snake (hiss).
The answer to the riddle is: **SOUND OFF.**

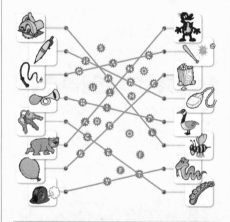

Write Off the Bat

The answer to the riddle is: **Every pitcher tells a story.**

Riddle Middle

The answer to the riddle is: **They both crack the case.**

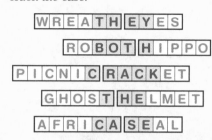

No Way!

The answer to the riddle is: POINTLESS.
The differences in the bottom picture, from left to right, are: bird's beak tip has more red; butterfly has a green spot; handle on chest changes; elephant's tusk is missing; explorer's hat has more sections; explorer's sleeve has a cuff added; knothole on tree is lower.

Dare to Compare

1. A hummingbird, which averages 3.4 grams. A nickel weighs 5 grams.
2. The cost of the movie, at almost $250 million. The ship cost $7.5 million.
3. The Statue of Liberty, completed in 1886. The Empire State Building was completed in 1931.
4. Asia, at 17.4 million square miles. The moon is 14.6 million square miles.
5. A blue whale, at up to 188 decibels, which can be heard over 500 miles away. A jackhammer gets up to 100 decibels. (Regular conversation is about 30 decibels.)

Sorry, Wrong Number

1. Low: 32 feet, 9.5 inches
2. High: 50 words
3. Low: 1,321 Earths
4. High: 26 Oscars
5. High: 12 letters
6. Low: 205 days
7. Low: 100 points

How Sweet It Is

The answer to the riddle is: DOUGH NUTS.
The differences in the bottom picture, from left to right, are: hard hat gets a visor; gumdrop on roof changes from yellow to blue; chimney changes on blueprint; crane's hook reverses direction; stripe on candy cane reverses direction; center of crane's wheel is bigger; light on crane's roof is missing.

Now Hear Hiss

The answer to the riddle is: He hasn't got a leg to stand on.

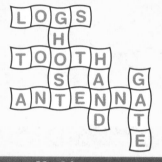

Sweet Nothings

The answer to the riddle is: Not a creature was stirring.

Ups and Downs

The answer to the riddle is: UMBRELLA.

175

Fair and Squares

The answer to the riddle is: **First prize was more pie.**

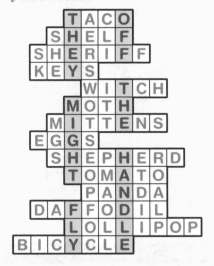

Cold Hard Facts

1. Porcupine—A porcupine may stay in its den during bad weather, but does not hibernate.
2. Snowmobiling—Ice dancing was introduced to the Olympics in 1976 and snowboarding in 1998.
3. Trees—Antarctica has a number of volcanoes and some small insects, but no plant life larger than lichen or moss.
4. They purr like cats—Polar bears growl, but they don't purr.
5. Its name means "Land of the Walrus"—"Alaska" comes from the Aleut word "alaxsxa," which translates loosely as "the mainland."
6. Fur earmuffs—The man, dubbed Ötzi by his discoverers, was found in the Alps in 1991.
7. Tundra—"Tundra" is a Russian word.
8. Fireworks display—So far, just one blind man has reached the top of Everest (in May 2001), and one wedding has taken place there (in June 2005).

Which Is Witch?

The answer to the riddle is: **They might fly off the handle.**

```
T A C O
S H E L F
S H E R I F F
K E Y S
      W I T C H
M O T H
M I T T E N S
E G G S
S H E P H E R D
T O M A T O
  P A N D A
D A F F O D I L
  L O L L I P O P
B I C Y C L E
```

Shooting Star

The answer to the riddle is:
IN THE CAST.

The differences in the bottom picture, from left to right, are: shoe is gone in poster; shirt collar is different; photograph of stuntman is reversed; pitcher is fuller; man has become bald; color of stripe on helmet is different; fuse is shorter.

Holiday Notes

The answer to the riddle is:
JUNGLE BELLS.

J O B S	G R I N
O V A L	R U D E
B A K E	I D E A
S L E D	N E A T

Break It Up!

The answer to the riddle is:
SHORTSTOP (SHORTS/TOP).

1. SIL VER
2. SHA DOW
3. WIN TER
4. BAT ONS
5. SPO NGE
6. CHA RTS
7. COU PON

Double Cross

The answer to the riddle is: **Because it was two in tents (too intense).**

Jokers Wild

The answer to the riddle is: **He had no scents of humor.**

The Inside Story

The pairs are: **ram/frame, top/octopus, hand/chandelier, star/mustard, bag/garbage, rat/pirate, cord/accordion, rake/parakeet.**
The answer to the riddle is: **DICTIONARY.**

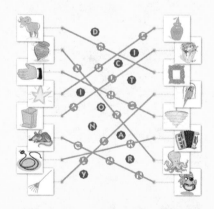

Double Space

The answer to the riddle is: **FIRED UP.**
The differences in the bottom picture, from left to right, are: **no glasses on tall man in monitor; hand control is lower; fingers on waving hand are separated; helmet has stripe; moon becomes Saturn in map; red light is yellow; buckle is missing; flag is turned; Earth is rotated.**

Monster Match

The answer to the riddle is: **They were made for each other.**

Treasure Jest

The answer is: **April fools.**

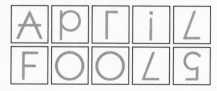

Witch You Were Here

The answer to the riddle is:
BROOM SERVICE.

Night Shift

The answer to the riddle is:
BUNK BEDS.

Tuning Out

1. Ring, king, spring
2. Bank, wand
3. Gears, bear, pear
4. Keys (piano keys and door keys)
5. Stone
6. Archer, gift, violin

The answer to the riddle is:
DRUMSTICKS.

For Starters

The pairs are: beak/beacon, tack/taxi, batter/battery, arm/armadillo, pencil/Pennsylvania, harp/harpoon, missile/mistletoe, pickle/piccolo.
The answer to the riddle is: YELLOW (YELL/OW).

Flying Colors

The answer to the riddle is: **They asked him for a hand.**

3: ALICE IN WANDERLAND

Island Hopping

Wrap Stars

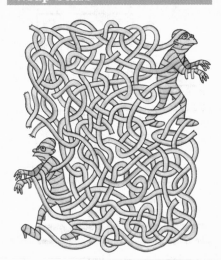

Are We There Yet?

Dashing Through the Snow

Go With the Flow

Potion in Motion

What Goes Around?

The correct path reads: What place has flies and bats and noisy fans, and people who might get caught stealing, and grown men running home, and a plate but no food, and a pitcher but no water?

The answer to the riddle is: A baseball stadium.

Bug Out

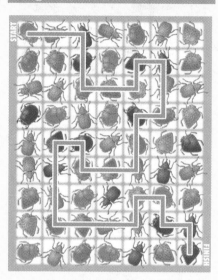

Flea Circuit

The Long Run

The completed path spells out the word GOLD.

Chicken Out

Web Search

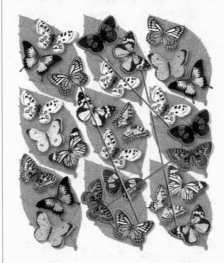

Garden Path

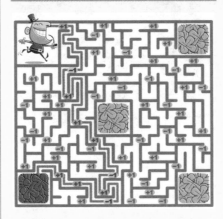

Bee Lines

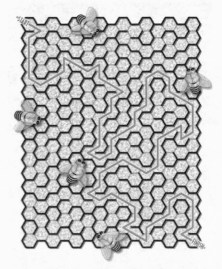

Stick Around

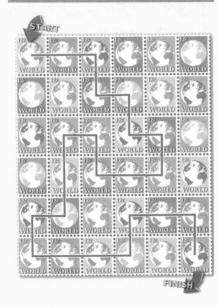

A Run of Luck

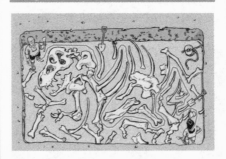

On the Word Path

Words from the correct path:
toothpick, pickpocket, pocket watch,
watchdog, doghouse, housefly,
flypaper, paperback, backfire,
firecracker, crackerjack, jackpot,
pothole.

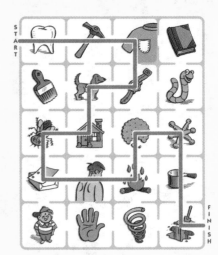

That's a Wrap!

Dig In!

Dead End

Hold Your Tongue!

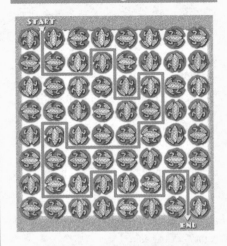

Floor Plan

Clearance Sail

Don't Go There

4: THE WORDMAN OF ALCATRAZ

Give Me a C! Give Me a D!

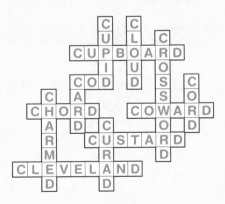

In the O Zone

Leftover message: **Top-notch job from top to bottom. Now go goof off.**

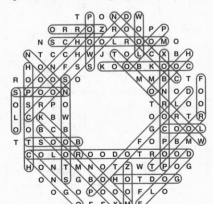

Hot Stuff

CAMP, DAMP, DUMP, LUMP, LIMP, LIME, DIME, DIVE, FIVE, FIRE

Tag Team

Top row: Heather/sweater, Stephanie/telephone, Ryan/crayons.
Bottom row: Nicole/unicycle, Christopher/microscope, Alexander/calendar.

Letter Openers

Scarecrow selling stamps, pirate pulling penguin, lumberjack licking lollipop, doctor dropping donuts, ballerina balancing boxes, witch weighing watermelon, judge juggling jars, vampire vacuuming valentines, mermaid mailing magnet, farmer folding flag, elephant eating envelopes, triplets taping tambourines.

Spellbound

TOAD, ROAD, ROAR, REAR, BEAR, BEAT, NEAT, NEWT

Hawaiian Tour

Leftover message: Ukulele actually means "leaping flea" in Hawaiian.

Chain of Command

Adams	Nixon
Madison	Clinton
Jackson	Washington
McKinley	Grant
Lincoln	Reagan

Catching Flies

Leftover message: You finished this with flying colors.

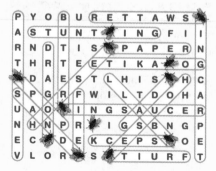

"In"strumental

Peter and Tippi had **sharply** different tastes in music. Peter liked to **sit around** in the **tub and** listen to jazz, while Tippi really **re**sponded to rock concerts.

One night, Tippi told Peter that she was planning **on** going to see her favorite band even though she'd heard **rum**ors that the concert was sold out. Her plan was to pack **a zoom** lens and a camera and blend in with all the paparazzi **there**.

"You think they're so dis**organ**ized, they let in every shutter**bug left** and right?" Peter asked.

Tippi said, "When I turn the **charm on I can** get past anyone."

"But tonight's ra**violi night**," Peter whined. "Would you really can**cel long**-standing plans?"

"Abso**lutely**!" she replied, and left.

Before long, Tippi returned and threw the biggest tan**trum Peter** had ever seen. The police had given Tip**pi an order** to go home for **violat**ing the law. Peter smiled as he said, "Will you feel better **if I fetch** you some cold ravioli?"

Odd Balls

1. Gumball
2. Handball
3. Basketball
4. Crystal ball
5. Football
6. Hair ball
7. Meatball
8. Pinball
9. Mothball

Drawing Blanks

The highlighted letters spell PICTURE PERFECT.

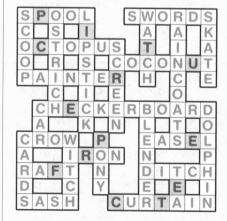

All Wet

1. Melon
2. Fall
3. Buffalo
4. Balloon
5. Polo
6. Colors
7. Slide
8. Skiing

Treat or Trick?

Riddle: Who is always the clear winner in Halloween games?
The answer to the riddle is: GHOST.

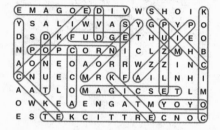

Laugh Tracks

Board Game

1. Keyboard
2. Clipboard
3. Backboard
4. Cardboard
5. Blackboard
6. Snowboard
7. Billboard

Easy as ABC

1. Apes Breaking Crayons
2. Ants Building Castle
3. Alice Buying Cherries
4. Angels Baking Cookies
5. Adam Balancing Cows
6. Astronauts Brushing Cats

Big Deal

Leftover message: Acorns and bells are German card suits.

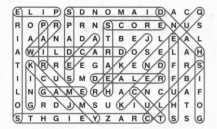

Small Change

1. Horse house
2. Plane plant
3. Sneaker speaker
4. Stork store
5. Leopard leotard
6. Soap soup
7. Chimp champ
8. Roman woman

Brain Storm

1. Rain
2. Ain't
3. Tear
4. Earth
5. Thunder
6. Undersea
7. Season
8. Sons
9. Spark
10. Parka
11. Abe
12. Before
13. Forecast
14. Castle
15. Lemon
16. Monsoon
17. Sooner

Outback Pack

Leftover message: Seven times as many sheep as people live in Australia.

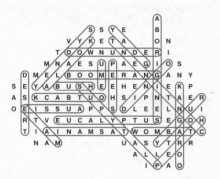

Body Building

Head: head of lettuce
Eyes: needle parts
Ears: ears of corn
Teeth: comb parts
Neck: bottle part
Heart: ace of hearts
Chest: treasure chest
Arms: axes
Hands: clock parts
Palms: palm trees
Legs: table parts
Foot: ruler

Boxing Match

The shaded columns read: **You can say that again.**
The leftover pictures are: yo-yo, dodo, and pom-pom.

Shore Enough

SAND, WAND, WIND, MIND, MINE, LINE, LANE, JANE, JUNE, DUNE

Pinwheel

Double Headers

The words are:

CALF	DONKEY
HALF	MONKEY
ITEM	CREASE
STEM	GREASE
FAULT	CHEATER
VAULT	THEATER
CHIEF	CRANIUM
THIEF	URANIUM
ALONE	CARRIAGE
CLONE	MARRIAGE
DUNCE	JAWBREAKER
OUNCE	LAWBREAKER

Leftover message: Hope you found this to be a great treat.

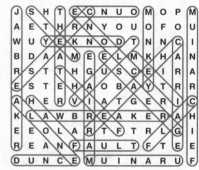

City Lines

Toledo	Honolulu
Detroit	Los Angeles
Baltimore	Las Vegas
Sacramento	Cleveland
Houston	Denver

Cold Spell

1. Shoes
2. Cone
3. Drift
4. White
5. Board
6. Ball
7. Storm

Scene of the Rhyme

Blizzard, lizard, wizard
Bunny, honey, money
Candle, handle (on briefcase), sandal
Coaster, poster, toaster
Flower, shower, tower
Label (on honey jar), stable, table

Same Hear!

Aloud—allowed	Soared—sword
Board—bored	Some—sum
Crews—cruise	Suite—sweet
Cymbal—symbol	Sun—son
Flower—flour	Threw—through
Grocer—grosser	Thrown—throne
Hire—higher	Toe—tow
Hoes—hose	Wait—weight
Kernel—colonel	Whether—
Patients—	weather
patience	Whirled—world
Peace—piece	Worn—warn
Role—roll	Would—wood
Sale—sail	

Leftover message: Seams ewe mist nun. (Seems you missed none.)

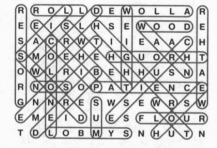

Get Packing

SNOW, SLOW, PLOW, PLOT, BLOT, BOOT, BOAT, BEAT, BELT, BELL, BALL

Veg Out

1. Beans (beings)
2. Turnip (turn up)
3. Carrot (care at)
4. Pepper (paper)
5. Lettuce (let us)
6. Peas (piece)
7. Cauliflower (call a flower)
8. Potatoes (put eight O's)

Open and Shut Case

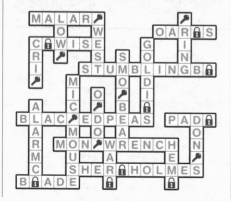

Keep It Down!

Leftover message: The blue whale is much louder than a plane.

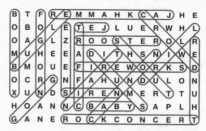

Crying Wolf

FULL, FALL, BALL, BELL, BELT, BOLT, BOAT, MOAT, MOAN, MOON

Is Everything OK?

Objects: Oven keys, orange kazoo, owl kimono, origami kangaroo, open ketchup, orangutan kilt, oily kayak, octopus king, oval kite, Olympic kitten, orbiting kettle, ostrich kiss, old kaleidoscope.

Knight Watch

Leftover message: Knights who can't defeat dragons get fired.

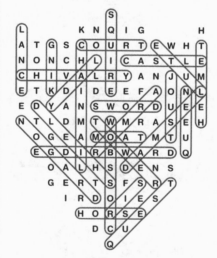

What in the World?

First column: Italy/whistle, Canada/sandals, Norway/snowboard, Hungary/hourglass.
Second column: Egypt/teapot, Sweden/sword, India/sundial, France/fan.

Sound Tracks

SOLO, SILO, SILK, SINK, PINK, PICK, PUCK, DUCK, DUSK, DUST, DUET

Spell Weaving

1. Spin	8. Trash
2. Pinch	9. Shallow
3. Chair	10. Allowance
4. Airplane	11. Ancestor
5. Planet	12. Storm
6. Torches	13. Master
7. Orchestra	14. Asteroid

Built to Order

Flurry	Icicle
Freeze	Shovel
Gloves	Winter

Mummy's the Word

Leftover message: King Tut's coffin is solid gold.

Incredible Edibles

1. Pear chair	5. Cake lake
2. Pickle nickel	6. Corn horn
3. Cheese skis	7. Jell-O cello
4. Frank tank	8. Bread bed

The Fright Stuff

1. Ghost	4. Goblin
2. Witch	5. Bat
3. Werewolf	6. Skeleton

Animal Tracks

Hyena	Crocodile
Elephant	Gorilla
Hippopotamus	Flamingo
Ostrich	Giraffe
Rhinoceros	Zebra

Give Us a Ring

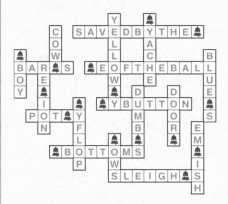

Make the Rounds

The Hole Story

Leftover message: The biggest man-made hole is a mine visible from space.

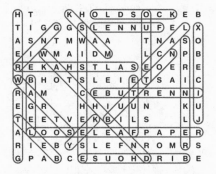

Play List

ROCK, SOCK, SICK, NICK, NICE, NINE, LINE, LANE, LAND, BAND

Diamond Hunt

The answer to the riddle is: She wanted to catch a fly.

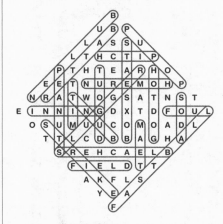

Ski Run

DOWN, DAWN, PAWN, PAWS, PALS, PALE, MALE, MALL, HALL, HILL

How's It Going?

1. Chimp blimp
2. Crab cab
3. Actor tractor
4. Dragon wagon
5. Bowler stroller
6. Shark ark
7. Sheep jeep
8. Collie trolley

This & That

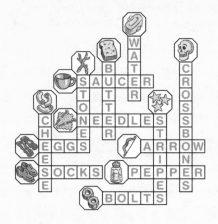

Get the Point?

Leftover message: We say we hang up when we put the phone down.

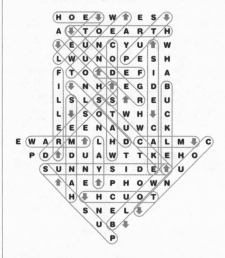

Fitting In

The shaded columns read: Wishful thinking.

The leftover pictures are: birthday cake, shooting star, and Aladdin's lamp (all things you wish on).

Flag Daze

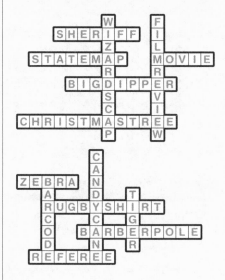

185

Jungle Jam

Leftover message: **Rain forests have half of Earth's species.**

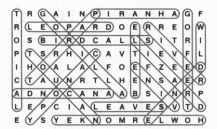

Play by Play

Flute	Saxophone
Tuba	Harmonica
Guitar	Tambourine
Triangle	Oboe
Piano	Trombone

Going Back on Your Word

1. Pool loop
2. Straw warts
3. Bus sub
4. Step pets
5. Star rats
6. Gum mug
7. Drawer reward
8. Stressed desserts

The Name of the Game

Blitz—football	Jab—boxing
Corner kick— soccer	Love—tennis
Dunk— basketball	Putt—golf
Headlock— wrestling	Safe—baseball
	Slap shot— hockey
	Spare—bowling

Leftover message: **Despite its nickname, a football isn't made of pigskin.**

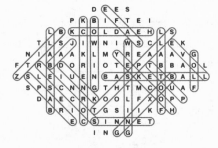

Long Shot

ZOOM, BOOM, BOOT, BOAT, BOAS, BOSS, LOSS, LOGS, LEGS, LENS

186

Runaround

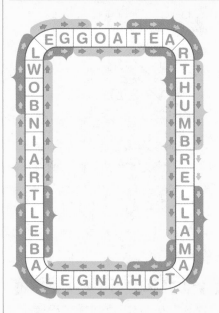

Going Wild

1. Fox (of **ox**ygen)
2. Beaver (**be a very**)
3. Rabbit (**grab bits**)
4. Otter (**got terr**ibly)
5. Bear (du**mb earflaps**)
6. Caribou (**car I bought**)
7. Elk (fe**el kind**)
8. Seal (lo**se a lot**)

Rated PG

Objects: **Pizza gong, pumpkin game, police gorilla, pet giraffe, painted guitar, purple grasshopper, Popsicle garden, pineapple glasses, peacock gown, pretzel glue, peanut globe, prize goldfish, pencil gate.**

Treasure Hunt

Leftover message: **Some pirates were women disguised as men.**

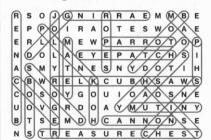

Batting Order

Roundabout

Home Sweet Home

Leftover message: **The tallest house of cards ever created measured about twenty-five feet.**

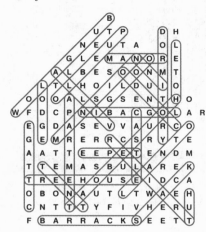

Mad About Hue

Objects: Blue jay, black widow, redhead, black belt, green beans, Yellow Pages, blue ribbon, blueberries, orange juice, white bread, Red Sox, Yellow Brick Road, red carpet, greenhouse, blue jeans, blackboard, blacksmith, black eye, yellow jacket, White Rabbit, blueprint, White House.

Sports Casting

Swimming	Archery
Gymnastics	Hockey
Tennis	Soccer
Wrestling	Lacrosse
Basketball	Baseball
Karate	

The White Album

The answer to the riddle is: **You look all white to me.**

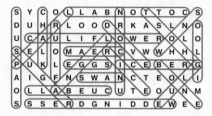

Else Wear

The costumes worn, plus the original costumes, are:

Purse (nurse)	Lizard (wizard)
Crown (clown)	Gelatin (skeleton)
Kite (knight)	Pear (bear)
Switch (witch)	Toast (ghost)

Man Hunt

Leftover message: **The only man you did not find here is the Invisible Man.**

The Nutty Professions

1. Preacher and teacher
2. Skater and waiter
3. Diver and driver
4. Charmer and farmer
5. Fighter and writer
6. Drummer and plumber
7. Sailor and tailor
8. Chef and ref

Music Boxes

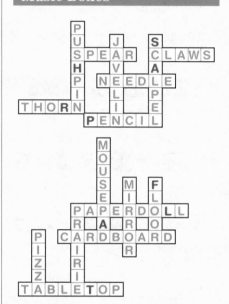

Word-Wide Web

Station Identification

Objects: Tired ventriloquist, trophy vault, taped vase, towed van, tall Viking, twisted violin, tomato volcano, tan volleyball, tattooed vampire, torn valentine, toasted vegetables, toy vulture, tiger vest.

Downpour

RAIN, PAIN, PAWN, PAWS, PATS, CATS, CUTS, HUTS, HUGS, HOGS, DOGS

No L, No L

2 L's:	3 L's:
Bully	Belly flop
Cello	Golf ball
Gazelle	Little League
Honolulu	Jingle Bells
Holly	Lollipop
Lilac	Lullaby
Lincoln	
Jolly	4 L's:
Mall	Hillbilly
Molecule	Volleyball
Lonely	
Pull	

Leftover message: **You need an L to sing "Fa la la la la."**

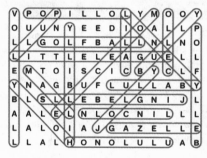

187

5: SHERLOGIC HOLMES

Under Wraps

1. Soccer ball
2. Scooter
3. Telescope
4. CD player
5. Guitar
6. Backpack
7. Video game
8. Mountain bike

Trick Question

The trick April wants is Snake in the Can.

Making a Scene

The correct order is: 6, 3, 1, 4, 5, 2.

Barking Lot

Dog 1 belongs to Francine.
Dog 2 belongs to Charlie.
Dog 3 belongs to Dora.
Dog 4 belongs to Beth.
Dog 5 belongs to Arnie.
Dog 6 belongs to Evan.

Making Faces

The correct order is: G, F (dad's and boy's heads switch), B (dog's ears and girl's ponytails switch), I (dad gets mustache from duplicated eyebrows), D (boy's head is enlarged), C (facial features of dog and girl switch), H (two neckties added), A (smiley face frowns), and E (mom's cowlick removed).

Wild Cards

The facedown card is the 5.

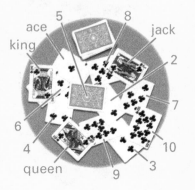

Join the Crowd

1. e (names of baseball teams: Pirates, Angels, Tigers, Twins)
2. b (things that go up and down: drawbridge, yo-yo, elevator, windowshade)
3. c (things made of wood: marionette, picnic table, baseball bat, pencil)
4. a (boys' names: Mike, Lance, Bill, Jack)
5. d (words ending in "o": flamingo, banjo, volcano, taco)

Stocking Stumpers

Holly's stocking is the second one from the left.

Shutterbug

The correct order is: 2, 6, 1, 5, 3, 4.

Your Move

1. Basketball
2. Fencing
3. Golf
4. Pool
5. Weight lifting
6. Bowling
7. Tennis
8. Volleyball
9. Football
10. Baseball
11. Archery
12. Figure skating

Taken For a Ride

Mom: Log flume
Dad: Hall of mirrors
Grandpa: Ferris wheel
Brother: Spinning teacups
Sister: Water slide
Grandma: Roller coaster

Pet Peeve

The correct order is: 3, 4, 1, 6, 2, 5.

Cool Customer

The sled Skip wants is the blue one with racing stripes that costs $32.

Reverse Gear

The items shown backward are: Big Dipper, Statue of Liberty, ace of spades, school crossing sign.

Floor It!

1. Bookcase
2. Wastebasket
3. Desk
4. Office chair
5. Speakers
6. Rug
7. Floor lamp
8. Welcome mat
9. Bed
10. Barbell
11. Suitcase
12. Door
13. In-line skates
14. Nightstand
15. Bike
16. Paint can

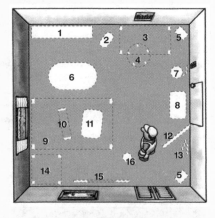

Wild Thing

The mildebeest is the gray animal at lower left standing on the tree trunk.

Hiding Places

1. California
2. Tokyo
3. Las Vegas
4. Egypt
5. Venice
6. Mississippi
7. Hawaii
8. New Orleans
9. Australia
10. Toronto
11. Philadelphia
12. Brazil

Scare Wear

The pirate is Pat.
The vampire is Taylor.
The one-eyed caveman is Alex.
The clown is Gerry.
The wizard is Jesse.
The ghost is Chris.

Fool Blast

The correct order is: 5, 3, 4, 1, 6, 2.

That's the Ticket!

The movie Mattie wants to see is *Nuts & Bolts*.

Letter Perfect

The leftover letters can be rearranged to spell YES.

P J V K U R
C T B Q A L
F M Z D G W
H N O X I

In the Present

The correct order is: 2, 4, 3, 6, 1, 5.

Fifty-Fifty Split

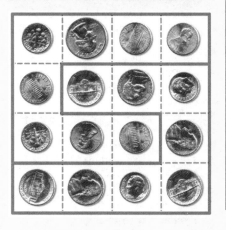

Ifs, Ands & 'Bots

The robot you want is Robot B.

Out of Order

The correct order is: 4, 6, 2, 1, 5, 3.

Size 'Em Up

Shown larger: penny, AA battery, eraser cap.

Shown smaller: Popsicle stick, crayon, CD.

Shown correct size: credit card, golf ball, quarter.

Sign Language

Ed's VCR Repair is in the style of The Sport Spot.

Granny's Toy House is in the style of Hardware Hut.

Comix is in the style of Granny's Toy House.

Hardware Hut is in the style of Paint City.

The Sport Spot is in the style of Takeout Taco.

Speedy Delivery is in the style of Ed's VCR Repair.

Paint City is in the style of Speedy Delivery.

Takeout Taco is in the style of Comix.

Snow Problem

Amelia: Snowman 2
Brad: Snowman 1
Caitlyn: Snowman 3
Drew: Snowman 4
Evan: Snowman 6
Faith: Snowman 5

Makeup Test

The correct order is: C, H, D, B, J, F, L, A, G, K, E, I.

Fish Story

The correct order is: 3, 6, 1, 5, 2, 4.

6: FRANKEINSTEIN

Rhyme and Season

Item pairs: Castle/tassel, tents/fence, bees/skis, hive/five, shed/sled, hoe/snow, cow/plow, racket/jacket, cat/hat, kittens/mittens, fountain/mountain, hair/bear, towel/owl, dollar/collar, shorts/forts, sandal/handle, tire/fire, axe/tracks, stump/pump, weights/skates, grass/glass, mice/ice, roots/boots, juice/moose, bicycle/icicle.

Take It or Leave It

1. HORSE + CAST − TORCH = SEAS
2. DART + EYES − TREE = DAYS
3. DUNCE + WATERMELON − TUNNEL + FISH − MICE − HOE = DWARFS

The answers are all things that come in groups of SEVEN.

Pole Vault

Face to Face

1-D, 2-E, 3-B, 4-C, 5-A

Afterwords

1. DENTIST
2. OPERATOR
3. EFFECTS
4. HISTORY
5. NOODLE
6. TURTLE
7. XYLOPHONE
8. STRAW
9. GHOST
10. KLUTZ

The answer to the riddle is: Because IT FOLLOWS U.

Three-for-Alls

1. Nest, nets, tens
2. Coast, coats, tacos
3. Inks, sink, skin
4. Art, rat, tar
5. Arms, rams, Mars
6. Petals, plates, staple

Take Your Pick

Peanut butter cup
Headphone jack
Horseshoe crab
Pancake batter
Basketball net

Gift Boxes

Animals: giraffe, iguana, frog, tiger, skunk
U.S. states: Georgia, Idaho, Florida, Texas, South Dakota
Parts of the body: gums, intestines, foot, tongue, skull
School supplies: glue, index cards, folder, tape, scissors
Leftover message: Now that you've got this puzzle all wrapped up, be sure to take a bow.

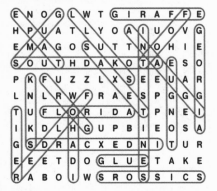

All Set

The sets are:
Things that spin (Earth, skater, top, CD)
Things you squeeze (rubber duck, toothpaste tube, accordion, sponge)
Things that have needles (compass, sewing machine, pine tree, doctor)
Words ending in X (fox, sphinx, mailbox, fax)

It All Adds Up

1. ROAD + BASKET = SKATEBOARD
2. ARM + DIME = MERMAID
3. NET + BROOM = TROMBONE
4. NURSE + WOLF = SUNFLOWER
5. SHIP + TURBAN = PAINTBRUSH
6. COOKIES + PEDAL = KALEIDOSCOPE

Get Cracking!

AT THE AMUSEMENT PARK

Roller coaster
Waterslide
Ferris wheel
Cotton candy
Skee-Ball
Merry-go-round
Fireworks show
Bumper cars
Fun house
Ticket booth

BLACK-AND-WHITE THINGS

Killer whale
Chess pieces
Old photograph
Eight ball
Skunk
Bar code
Crossword puzzle
Zebra
Ace of spades
Piano keys

Snow Way

Switcheroos

1. Bunny moat; money boat
2. Carrot petals; parrot kettles
3. Cat fight; fat kite
4. Crossed tickets; tossed crickets
5. Poodle knot; noodle pot
6. Shocked leopard; locked shepherd

Hear Here

1. plane, plain
2. week, weak
3. hour, our
4. isle, I'll
5. sea, see
6. whether, weather
7. ate, eight
8. sun, son
9. wear, where
10. weigh, way
11. sundae, Sunday
12. bored, board
13. know, no
14. grease, Greece

Common Sense

1. Shells
2. Trunks
3. Rings
4. Teeth
5. Poles
6. Tails
7. Bows
8. Blades

Hex Mix

T + carrot = tractor
P + pliers = slipper
A + pencil = pelican
O + crab = cobra
R + boot = robot
H + acorn = anchor

Letterheads

1. Enclosing (N closing)
2. Jaywalking (J walking)
3. Erasing (E racing)
4. Devoting (D voting)
5. Seesawing (C sawing)
6. Exchanging (X changing)
7. Believing (B leaving)

Spinning Wheel

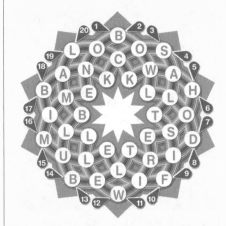

Think Twice

The answers, in order of the clues, are:

SQUIRREL	BEDROOM
GREEN	TRAFFIC
BUBBLE	PIZZERIA
WATERFALL	JOGGING
CHESSBOARD	OPPOSITES
COMMA	CHANNEL
BOTTLE	LADDER

The answer to the riddle is: When he BEGAN TO C DOUBLE.

Rhyme Wave

Peel, wheel/tire, fire/flame, game/board, cord/plug, mug/cup, up/arrow, sparrow/bird, herd/cattle, rattle/snake, steak/meat, seat/chair, hair/wig, pig/hog, frog/toad, road/street, feet/toes, rose/flower, shower/rain, chain.

Shore Thing

The correct order is: C, E, B, H, F, D, A, G.

Drop by Drop

1. Brush, bush, bus
2. Horse, hose, hoe
3. Canoe, cane, can
4. Scarf, scar, car
5. Chart, cart, cat
6. Beard, bear, ear
7. Paints, pants, ants
8. Prince, price, rice

Rhyme Spree

The rhyming words in the clues are:

1. Duller
2. Mammal
3. Locker
4. Hassle
5. Practice
6. Catches
7. Stencil
8. Tone
9. Treat
10. Boos
11. Goo
12. Male
13. Note
14. Knowledge
15. Find
16. Vital

Round Trip

BACK, BUCK, PUCK, PICK, LICK, LINK, LINE, MINE, MANE, CANE, CANS, CARS, CARD, YARD, YARN, BARN, BARK

Wild Flowers

1. Iris
2. Rose
3. Daisy
4. Violet
5. Tulip
6. Lily

Driving Wild

The answer to the riddle is: DOUBLE YELLOW LIONS.

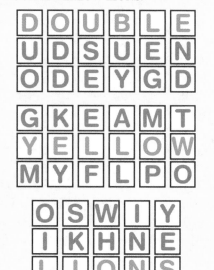

Way to Go

Truck	Tricycle
Scooter	Chariot
Stagecoach	Helicopter
Tractor	Canoe
Racecar	Airplane

Let It Snow

Presents and Absence

Each answer gives the wanted gift followed by the received gift and the missing letter.

1. Bridge, bride (G)
2. Tuba, tub (A)
3. Blackboard, backboard (L)
4. Bowl, owl (B)
5. Stairs, stars (I)
6. Crown, crow (N)
7. Flock, lock (F)
8. Raft, rat (F)

The missing letters can be unscrambled to spell BAFFLING.

Jeepers! Peepers!

View 7 is the view from your eyes as you solve the puzzle.

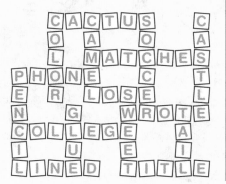

On the Contrary

Hard: easy, soft
Lie: stand, truth
Light: dark, heavy
Lost: found, won
Old: new, young
Poor: excellent, rich
Positive: negative, unsure
Right: left, wrong
Safe: dangerous, out
Short: long, tall
Leftover message: Well done!
(The opposite of rare.)

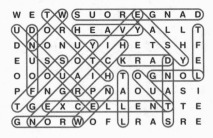

Gray Matter

The answer to the riddle is: They are scared of the mouse.

Box Sets

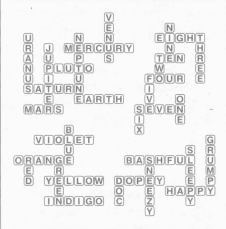

Get the Picture?

When you turn the painting on its side, the objects look like letters that spell out APRIL FOOLS.

"At last our long journey has been rewarded with the answers we sought."

"Finally I know my rights _and_ my wrongs!"

"Mmmmm ... answers good!"

"Of course! The solutions were hiding in the back all along!"

"I must say, I _had_ been getting curiouser and curiouser!"

"We will now release your pathetic planet from our riddling grip."